Math Connects 1

Problem-Solving Practice Workbook

Macmillan McGraw-Hill

Macmillan/McGraw-Hill

TO THE TEACHER These worksheets are the same ones found in the Chapter Resource Masters for *Math Connects, Grade 1*. The answers to these worksheets are available at the end of each Chapter Resource Masters booklet.

The McGraw·Hill Companies

Macmillan/McGraw-Hill

Copyright © by the McGraw-Hill Companies, Inc. All rights reserved. Except as permitted under the United States Copyright Act, no part of this publication may be reproduced or distributed in any form or by any means, or stored in a database or retrieval system, without prior written permission of the publisher.

Send all inquiries to:
Macmillan/McGraw-Hill
8787 Orion Place
Columbus, OH 43240

ISBN: 978-0-02-107288-0
MHID: 0-02-107288-4　　　　　*Problem-Solving Practice Workbook, Grade 1*

Printed in the United States of America.

2 3 4 5 6 7 8 9 10　021　14 13 12 11 10 09 08

CONTENTS

Chapter 1 Describe and Compare Numbers
- 1-1 Extend a Pattern 1
- 1-2 Create a Pattern 2
- 1-4 Numbers to 10 3
- 1-5 Numbers 11 to 15 4
- 1-6 Numbers 16 to 20 5
- 1-8 Compare Numbers 6
- 1-9 Order Numbers 7

Chapter 2 Develop Addition Concepts
- 2-1 Addition Stories 8
- 2-2 Modeling Addition 9
- 2-3 Addition Sentences 10
- 2-4 Adding Zero 11
- 2-6 Ways to Make 4, 5, and 6 12
- 2-7 Ways to Make 7, 8, and 9 13
- 2-8 Ways to Make 10, 11, and 12 14
- 2-10 Vertical Addition 15

Chapter 3 Develop Subtraction Concepts
- 3-1 Subtraction Stories 16
- 3-2 Modeling Subtraction 17
- 3-3 Subtraction Sentences 18
- 3-4 Subtract Zero and All 19
- 3-6 Subtract from 4, 5, and 6 20
- 3-7 Subtract from 7, 8, and 9 21
- 3-9 Subtract from 10, 11, and 12 22
- 3-10 Vertical Subtraction 23

Chapter 4 Organize and Use Data
- 4-1 Sort and Classify 24
- 4-2 Picture Graphs 25
- 4-4 Tally Charts 26
- 4-5 Read a Bar Graph 27
- 4-6 Make a Bar Graph 28
- 4-8 Certain or Impossible 29

Chapter 5 Develop Addition Strategies
- 5-1 Add in Any Order 30
- 5-2 Count On 1, 2, or 3 31
- 5-4 Add 1, 2, or 3 32
- 5-5 Use a Number Line to Add 33
- 5-6 Doubles 34
- 5-7 Doubles Plus 1 35

Chapter 6 Develop Subtraction Strategies
- 6-1 Count Back 1, 2, or 3 36
- 6-3 Use a Number Line to Subtract 37
- 6-5 Use Doubles to Subtract 38
- 6-6 Relate Addition to Subtraction 39
- 6-7 Fact Families 40

Chapter 7 Measure Time
- 7-1 Ordering Events 41
- 7-2 Time to the Hour 42
- 7-3 Time to the Half Hour 43
- 7-5 Telling Time to the Hour and Half Hour . . . 44
- 7-6 Relate Time to Events 45

Chapter 8 Recognize Number Patterns
- 8-1 Counting to 20 46
- 8-2 Counting by Tens 47
- 8-4 Hundred Chart 48
- 8-5 Estimating With Groups of Tens 49
- 8-7 Skip Counting by 2s, 5s, and 10s 50
- 8-8 Skip Counting on a Hundred Chart 51
- 8-9 Even and Odd 52

Chapter 9 Compare Measurements
- 9-1 Compare and Order Lengths 53
- 9-2 Nonstandard Units of Length 54
- 9-4 Compare and Order Weights 55
- 9-5 Compare and Order Capacities 56
- 9-6 Compare and Order Temperatures 57
- 9-8 Compare Areas 58
- 9-9 Order Areas 59

Chapter 10 Solve Addition and Subtraction Problems
- 10-1 Doubles 60
- 10-2 Doubles Plus 1 61
- 10-3 Make a 10 to Add 62
- 10-5 Use Doubles to Subtract 63
- 10-6 Relate Addition and Subtraction 64
- 10-8 Fact Families 65
- 10-9 Ways to Model Numbers 66

Chapter 11 Identify Coins
- 11-1 Pennies and Nickels 67
- 11-2 Pennies and Dimes 68
- 11-3 Pennies, Nickels, and Dimes 69
- 11-4 Counting Money 70
- 11-6 Equal Amounts 71
- 11-7 Quarters 72
- 11-9 Money Amounts 73

Chapter 12 Identify Geometric Figures

- 12-1 Three-Dimensional Figures 74
- 12-2 Faces and Corners 75
- 12-4 Two- and Three-Dimensional Figures 76
- 12-5 Two-Dimensional Figures 77
- 12-7 Make New Figures 78
- 12-8 Position 79
- 12-9 Give and Follow Directions 80

Chapter 13 Understand Place Value

- 13-1 Tens 81
- 13-2 Tens and Ones 82
- 13-4 Numbers to 50 83
- 13-5 Numbers to 100 84
- 13-6 Estimate Numbers 85
- 13-8 Compare Numbers to 100 86
- 13-9 Order Numbers to 100 87

Chapter 14 Describe Fractional Parts

- 14-1 Equal Parts 88
- 14-3 One Half 89
- 14-4 One Third and One Fourth 90
- 14-5 Non-Unit Fractions 91
- 14-6 Fractions of a Set 92

Chapter 15 Solve Two-Digit Addition and Subtractions Problems

- 15-1 Add and Subtract Tens 93
- 15-2 Add with Two-Digit Numbers 94
- 15-4 Add Two-Digit Numbers 95
- 15-5 Estimate Sums 96
- 15-6 Subtract with Two-Digit Numbers 97
- 15-7 Subtract Two-Digit Numbers 98
- 15-9 Estimate Differences 99

1-1

Name _____

Problem-Solving Practice

Extend a Pattern

Use a pattern to solve.

1. Bob makes a bracelet. It looks like this:

   Draw the next two beads.

2. Min draws a border. It looks like this:

   Draw the next two shapes.

3. Leon makes this pattern. Show his pattern with letters.

   ____ ____ ____ ____ ____ ____

4. Rosa makes this pattern. Show her pattern with letters.

   ____ ____ ____ ____ ____ ____

5. Cass draws a pattern. It looks like this:

   Owen guesses a circle is next. Is he correct?

   ____

6. Juan uses a pattern to hang up his family's coats. He hangs the coats in this order: Mom's coat, Dad's coat, Juan's coat, Mom's coat. What are the next two coats?

   _____

   _____

Grade 1

1

Chapter 1

1-2

Name _____

Problem-Solving Practice

Create a Pattern

Use pattern blocks to solve. Draw your answer.

1. Jon has 3 blocks: △, □, and ○. He makes this pattern unit:

   □ ○ △

   What other pattern unit can Jon make?

   Draw here.

2. Lu has 4 blocks: ○, □, △, and ▭. She makes this pattern unit:

   ○ □ △ ▭

   What other pattern unit can Lu make?

3. Kim has 3 blocks: a square, a rectangle, and a circle.

   She made this pattern:

   ○ □ ▭ ○ □ ▭

   What is one other pattern Kim can make?

Grade 1   Chapter 1

1-4

Name _____

Problem-Solving Practice

Numbers to 10

Read the directions. Write the answer.

1. Draw 3 ☼.

2. Count. Then draw lines to show how many.

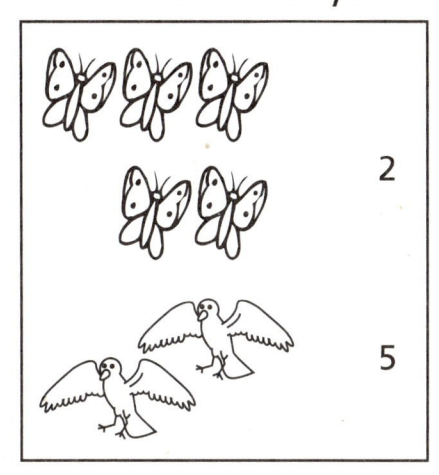

   2

   5

Count. Write the number.

3. 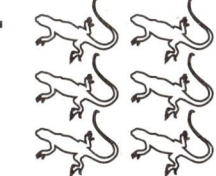 _____   4.  _____   5. 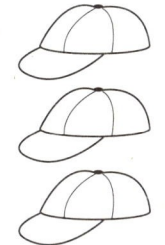 _____   6. _____

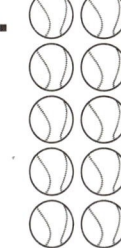

7. Color 2 stars red. Color the rest blue.

8. Number the stars. How many stars in all?

_____

☆ ☆ ☆ ☆ ☆ ☆ ☆ ☆

___ ___ ___ ___ ___ ___ ___ ___

Grade 1   3   Chapter 1

1-5

Name _____

Problem-Solving Practice

Numbers 11 to 15

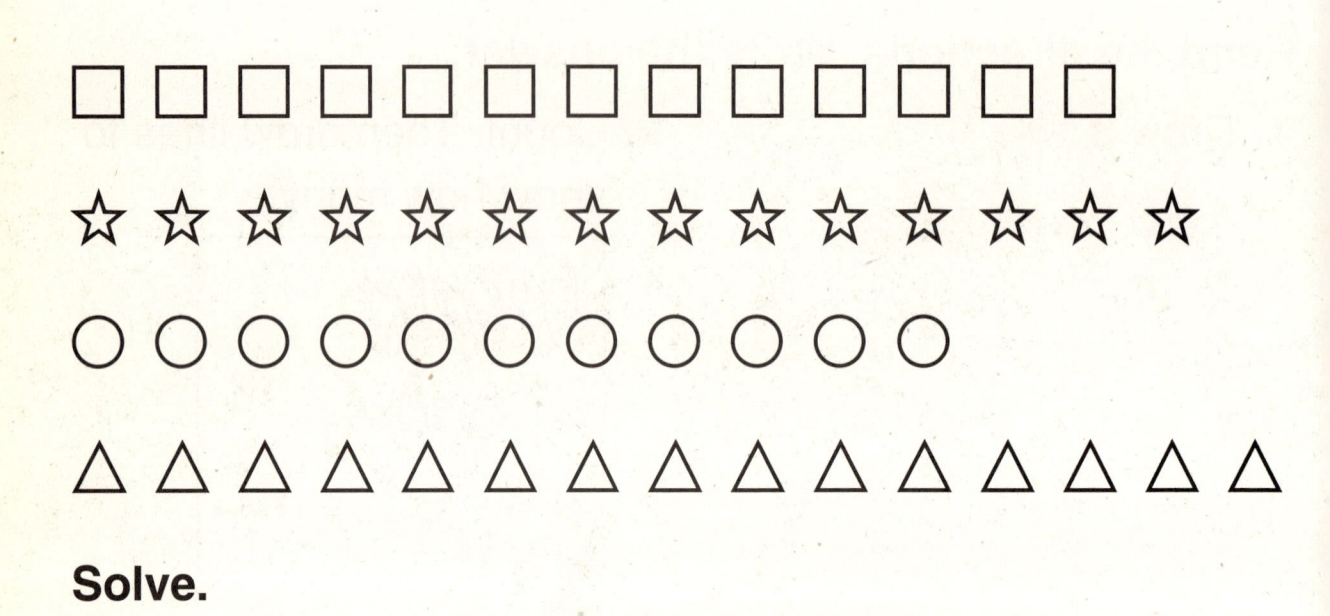

☐ ☐ ☐ ☐ ☐ ☐ ☐ ☐ ☐ ☐ ☐ ☐ ☐

☆ ☆ ☆ ☆ ☆ ☆ ☆ ☆ ☆ ☆ ☆ ☆ ☆ ☆

○ ○ ○ ○ ○ ○ ○ ○ ○ ○ ○

△ △ △ △ △ △ △ △ △ △ △ △ △ △ △

Solve.

1. Jen counts the △. How many does she count?

    _____ triangles

2. Rafi counts the ○. How many does he count?

    _____ circles

3. Leo counts ☆. How many does he count?

    _____ stars

4. Phil counts ☐. How many does he count?

    _____ squares

5. How many more ☆ than ☐?

    _____ star

6. How many more △ than ○?

    _____ triangles

Grade 1   4   Chapter 1

1-6 Problem-Solving Practice

Numbers 16 to 20

Count to solve. For 1–2, write the number and number word.

1. Tim has this many eggs:

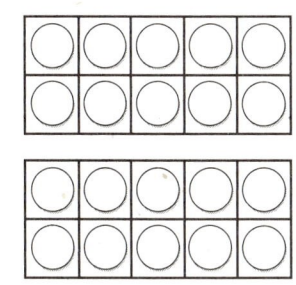

What number shows how many eggs? _____

What word shows how many eggs?

_____

2. Cho has this many eggs:

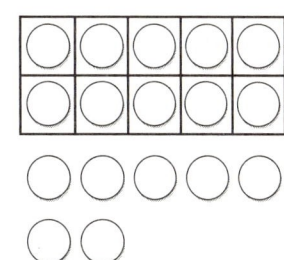

What number shows how many eggs? _____

What word shows how many eggs?

_____

3. Joe has ⬚⬚⬚⬚⬚ and ○○○○○○.

He has 1 ten and 6 ones. What is the number?

10   12   16

4. Lee wrote **eighteen** on her paper.

What number did she write?

13   18   20

Grade 1   Chapter 1

1-8

Name _____

Problem-Solving Practice
Compare Numbers

Solve.

1. Lee and Kal compare eggs.

   Lee's eggs   Kal's eggs

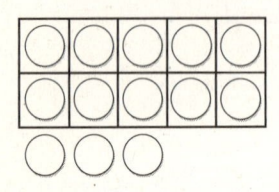

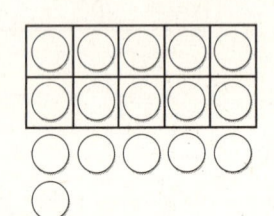

   Who has more eggs?
   _____

2. Anne and Lisa compare coins.

   Anne's coins   Lisa's coins

   Who has fewer coins?
   _____

3. Circle **greater** or **less**.
   Liz has 15 oranges.
   Her brother has 12.
   15 is _____ than 12.

   greater   less

4. Jack wrote these sentences. Draw an X next to each sentence that is true.

   15 is more than 10. ____
   13 is more than 15. ____
   29¢ is less than 31¢. ____

5. What number is more than 20 but less than 22?

   _____

Grade 1   6   Chapter 1

1-9

Name _____

Problem-Solving Practice

Order Numbers

Use the number line.

1 2 3 4 5 6 7 8 9 10 11 12 13 14 15 16 17 18 19 20

1. Circle the number that comes just **before** 8.

2. Draw a square around the number that comes just **after** 2.

3. Write the numbers that are missing.

   17, _____, 19,

   _____, 12, 13

4. What number comes **after** 16 and **before** 18?

   _____

5. Help Maria write her numbers in order.

Maria
○
12 19 8 17 14
○

   _____, _____, _____, _____, _____

Grade 1   Chapter 1

2-1

Name _____

Problem-Solving Practice

Addition Stories

Draw a picture to show how many in all.

1. Show 3 balls.
   Show 2 more.
   How many total balls?

   _____

2. Show 6 balls.
   Show 2 more.
   How many in all?

   _____

3. Sam has 3 cats.
   Amy has 2 cats.
   How many total cats?

   _____

4. The dog has 7 bones. He gets 3 more bones. How many bones altogether?

   _____

5. Doug and Mike play catch. Paul and Anna join them. How many total children are playing catch?

   _____

6. 9 children are at the party. 3 more children come. How many children are there in all?

   _____

2-2

Name _____

Problem-Solving Practice

Modeling Addition

Write how many in all. Use ●○.

1. Show 3.
   Add 2 more.
   How many altogether?

   _____

2. Show 2.
   Add 4 more.
   How many total?

   _____

3. 2 chickens are in the coop.
   5 more chickens are in the yard.
   How many chickens altogether?

   _____ chickens

4. 6 pigs are in the barn.
   2 more pigs are in the mud.
   How many pigs in all?

   _____ pigs

5. There are 8 roses blooming on a bush.
   2 more roses bloom the next day.
   How many total roses?

   _____ roses

6. Mia picks 7 flowers.
   Tim picks 1 more flower and gives it to Mia.
   How many flowers does Mia have in all?

   _____ flowers

Grade 1   Chapter 2

2-3

Name _____

Problem-Solving Practice
Addition Sentences

Circle or write the addition sentence.

1. Write two addition sentences that match the picture.

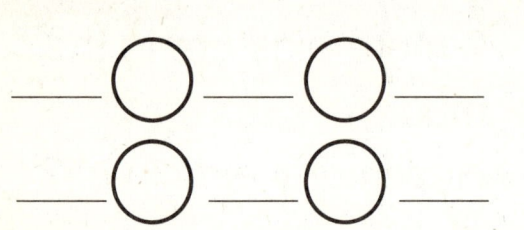

   ___ ◯ ___ ◯ ___

   ___ ◯ ___ ◯ ___

2. The picture shows 4 plus 2 equals 6. Write the addition sentence.

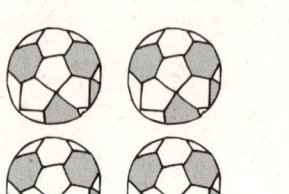

   ___ ◯ ___ ◯ ___

3. 2 plus 3 equals 5.

   ___ ◯ ___ ◯ ___

4. 7 plus 3 equals 10.

   ___ ◯ ___ ◯ ___

5. The cub eats 2 berries. Then he eats 8 more. How many berries does he eat in all?

   2 plus 8 equals 10.

   ___ ◯ ___ ◯ ___

6. 4 cubs play. 4 more join them. How many cubs in all?

   4 plus 4 equals 8.

   ___ ◯ ___ ◯ ___

Grade 1   Chapter 2

2-4

Name _____

Problem-Solving Practice

Adding Zero

Write the addition sentence to solve.

1.

   2 + 0 = ____

2.

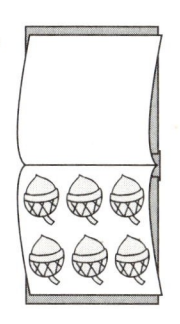

   $$\begin{array}{r} 0 \\ + 6 \\ \hline \end{array}$$

3.

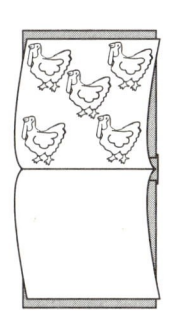

   ____ + ____

4.

   ____ + ____ = ____

5. There are 0 leaves on the left page. There are 3 leaves on the right page. How many leaves in all?

   ____ + ____ = ____

6. There are 4 stickers on the top page and 0 stickers on the bottom page. How many stickers in all?

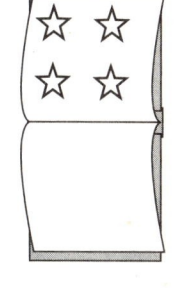

   ____ + ____ = ____

Grade 1   11   Chapter 2

2-6

Name _____

Problem-Solving Practice

Ways to Make 4, 5, and 6

Make 4, 5, and 6. Write the numbers and solve.

1. Josie has 2 🪙.
   Micky has 2 🪙.
   How many 🪙?

   ___ + ___ = 4 🪙

2. Sam has 3 🎾.
   May has 1 🎾.
   How many 🎾 altogether?

   ___ + ___ = 4 🎾

3. Win has 3 🦕.
   Trey has 2 🦕.
   How many 🦕 total?

   ___ + ___ = 5 🦕

4. Kay jumps 1 time.
   Gail jumps 5 times.
   How many times did they jump in all?

   ___ + ___ = 6 jumps

5. Sara buys 4 plums.
   John buys 2 plums.
   How many total plums did they buy?

   ___ + ___ = ___ plums

6. 3 friends are playing.
   2 more friends join them.
   How many friends play?

   ___ + ___ = ___ friends

Grade 1   Chapter 2

2-7

Name _____

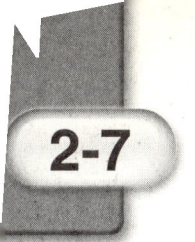

Problem-Solving Practice

Ways to Make 7, 8, and 9

Write the numbers and solve.

1. Eve has 3 .
   Bess has 4 .
   How many altogether?

   ___ + ___ = 7

2. Andy has 5 .
   Lin has 2 .
   How many in all?

   ___ + ___ = 7

3. 5 take off.
   3 wait in line.
   How many are there total?

   ___ + ___ = 8

4. Pia put together 4 trains. Morgan put 5 trains together.
   How many trains did they put together in all?

   ___ + ___ = ___ trains

5. 6 children like the color blue. 3 children like the color green.
   How many children like blue or green?

   ___ + ___ = ___ children

6. 4 children play tag. 4 more children join them.
   How many children are playing now?

   ___ + ___ = ___ children

Grade 1   13   Chapter 2

2-8

Name _____

Problem-Solving Practice

Ways to Make 10, 11, and 12

Draw or write addition sentences.

1. Draw a picture to show $2 + 8 = 10$.

2. Tina walks 4 blocks to school. Luis walks 7 blocks. How many blocks do they walk in all?

   _____ + _____ = _____

3. Carmen counts 4 red cars in the parking lot. Then she counts 8 black cars. How many total cars does she count?

   _____ + _____ = _____

4. 2 boys get on the bus. 9 more boys join them. How many boys are on the bus now?

   _____ + _____ = _____

5. 10 children are outside. Some sit on a bench. Others sit on the grass. Write one way the children could be sitting.

   _____ + _____ = _____

6. 12 children are on the bus. Some sit on the right side. Others sit on the left side. Write one way the children could be sitting.

   _____ + _____ = _____

Grade 1   14   Chapter 2

2-10 Name _____

Problem-Solving Practice
Vertical Addition

Draw a picture. Solve.

Sam has 4 apples.
Dan has 2 apples.

1. Use the picture. How many apples in all?

   _____ apples

2. Write the number fact across and down to tell the story.

   ____ + ____ = ____

Write two addition sentences.

3. Joe saw 5 seals at the zoo. Sue saw 3 bears. How many animals did they see in all?

   ____ + ____ = ____

4. Jill drew 7 stars. Then she drew 2 more. How many stars in all?

   ____ + ____ = ____

5. Jerry found 3 bugs. Pablo found 2 more. How many bugs did they find in all?

6. Carla has 6 stickers. Tina has none. How many stickers do they have in all?

Grade 1   15   Chapter 2

3-1

Name _____

Problem-Solving Practice

Subtraction Stories

**Tell a number story.
Use ◯. Write how many are left.**

1. There were 5 balls.
   We lost 2.
   How many are left?

   _____

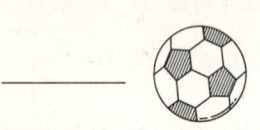

2. Show 6 balls.
   Take away 2.
   How many are left?

   _____

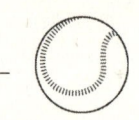

3. Sam's cat had 6 kittens.
   He gave away 4.
   How many now?

   _____

4. The dog has 7 bones.
   He eats 3 bones.
   How many are left?

   _____

5. Doug, Mike, Paul, and
   Anna play catch.
   Then Paul and Anna
   went home.
   How many children are
   left?

   _____

6. 9 children come
   to the party.
   3 children leave.
   How many children
   are left at the party?

   _____

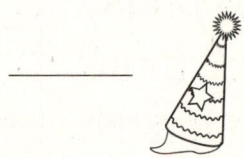

3-2

Name _____

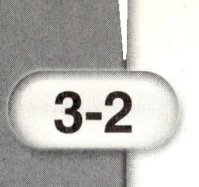

Problem-Solving Practice

Modeling Subtraction

**Use WorkMat 3 and ◯ to subtract.
Write how many are left.**

1. Show 10.
   Take away 7.
   How many are left?

   _____

   10 take away 7 is _____.

2. Show 4.
   Take away 3.
   How many now?

   _____

   4 take away 3 is _____.

3. There are 9 ◯ in all.
   Take away 1.
   How many ◯ now?

   _____

   9 take away 1 is _____.

4. There are 7 ◯ in all.
   Take away 1.
   How many ◯ are left?

   _____

   7 take away 1 is _____.

5. Jess has 7 tickets.
   She sells 2.
   How many tickets does she have left?

   _____

   7 take away 2 is _____.

6. Lou has 10 stickers.
   He puts 2 on his door.
   How many stickers now?

   _____

   10 take away 2 is _____.

Grade 1   Chapter 3

3-3

Name _____

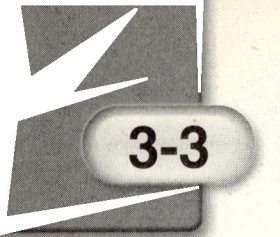

Problem-Solving Practice

Subtraction Sentences

Write the subtraction sentence.

1. 9 take away 2 is ___.

    ___ ◯ ___ ◯ ___

2. 5 take away 3 is ___.

    ___ ◯ ___ ◯ ___

3. 6 take away 2 is ___.

    ___ ◯ ___ ◯ ___

4. 5 take away 1 is ___.

    ___ ◯ ___ ◯ ___

5. 10 take away 5 is ___.

    ___ ◯ ___ ◯ ___

6. 9 take away 6 is ___.

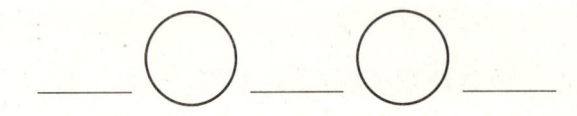

    ___ ◯ ___ ◯ ___

7. Kay sees 10 ducks.
   7 ducks fly away.
   How many ducks are left?

   10 take away 7 is ___.

   ___ ◯ ___ ◯ ___

8. There are 7 cows.
   2 cows are brown.
   How many cows are *not* brown?

   7 take away 2 is ___.

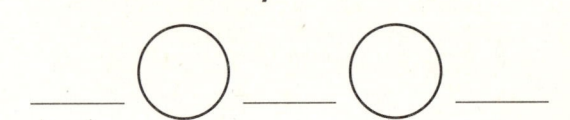

   ___ ◯ ___ ◯ ___

Grade 1   18   Chapter 3

3-4

Name _____

Problem-Solving Practice

Subtract Zero and All

Find the difference. Use ◯ if needed.

1. Mindy has 3 🧁.
   She eats them all.
   How many 🧁 does she have left?

   3 − 3 = _____

2. Kyle has 10 🍎.
   He does not eat any of them.
   How many 🍎 does he have left?

   10 − 0 = _____

3. There are six cows in the pen.
   Zero cows went in the barn.
   How many cows are in the pen?

   6 − 0 = _____

4. Tanya has 10 crayons.
   She gives some to Kim.
   Tanya has no more crayons.
   How many crayons did Tanya give to Kim?

   10 − _____ = 0

Write the number sentence.

5. I ate all the brownies.
   There were 7 in all.
   How many brownies do I have now?

   _____

6. I cut 8 pieces of cheese.
   No one ate them.
   How many pieces of cheese do I have left?

   _____

Grade 1　　19　　Chapter 3

3-6

Name _____

Problem-Solving Practice

Subtract from 4, 5, and 6

Find the difference. Write the numbers.

1. Draw 6 ☺.
   Cross out 4.
   Write the numbers.
   6 – ____ = ____

2. Draw 5 ☺.
   Cross out 2.
   Write the numbers.
   5 – ____ = ____

3. Phil draws 5 ☺.
   He erases 1.
   How many are left?
   5 – ____ = ____

4. Abby draws 7 ☺.
   She crosses out 2.
   How many are there now?
   7 – ____ = ____

5. Josie draws 6 ☺.
   She erases 2.
   How many are left?
   ____ – ____ = ____

6. Billy draws 6 ☺.
   He crosses out 1.
   How many are there now?
   6 – ____ = ____

Grade 1 — Chapter 3

3-7

Name _____

Problem-Solving Practice

Subtract from 7, 8, and 9

Find the difference. Write the numbers.

1. 7 − 2 = _____

2. 9 − 4 = _____

Write the subtraction sentence.

3. Jorge puts 9 shirts in a box.
   He takes out 3.
   How many shirts are still in the box?

   9 − _____ = _____ shirts

4. Maria puts 7 books in her desk.
   She takes out 3.
   How many books are left in her desk?

   7 − _____ = _____ books

5. Maria has 9 pennies.
   She uses 5 to buy a piece of gum.
   How many pennies does Maria have left?

   _____ − _____ = _____

6. It is 9 miles to the airport.
   Dad drives 3.
   How many more miles does Dad have to drive?

   _____ − _____ = _____

Grade 1　　　21　　　Chapter 3

3-9

Name _____

Problem-Solving Practice

Subtract from 10, 11, and 12

Draw a picture. Find the difference.

1. Draw 10 △. Take away 2. The difference is ____

2. Draw 12 □. Take away 4. The difference is ____

Solve.

3. 11 children wait in line. 5 children get on the ride. How many children are still waiting?

   11 − 5 = ____ children

4. Jody has 10 chances to hit the bell. She has tried 7 times. How many chances does she have?

   10 − 7 = ____ chances

Write a subtraction sentence.

5. Mrs. Jones has 12 tickets. She gives some away. Mrs. Jones still has 6 tickets. How many did she give away?

   ____ − ____ = ____

6. There are 11 children sitting on a bench. 3 go home. How many children are still on the bench?

   ____ − ____ = ____

Grade 1   Chapter 3

3-10

Name _____

Problem-Solving Practice

Vertical Subtraction

Write two subtraction sentences. Solve.

1. 7 penguins are on the ice. 4 penguins jump in the water. How many penguins are left on the ice? _____ penguins

   ____ − ____ = ____

2. There are 10 pieces of pizza. Lara eats 2 pieces. How many pieces are left?

   ____ − ____ = ____

3. Sela has 9 cookies. She gives 4 cookies to Raul. How many cookies does Sela have left?

   ____ − ____ = ____

Solve.

4. Yoko has 8 books. She gives 2 books to her brother and 3 books to her sister.

   How many books does she have left? _____ books

5. Jen has 5 apples. 3 apples are green. How many apples are *not* green? _____ apples

Grade 1   Chapter 3

4-1

Name _____

Problem-Solving Practice

Sort and Classify

Solve.

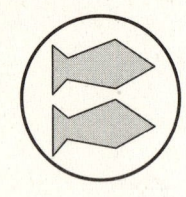

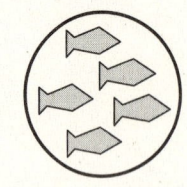

1. How are the fish sorted?

   size shape

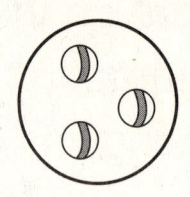

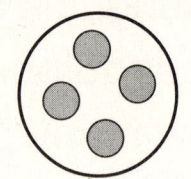

2. How are the balls sorted?

   size pattern

3. Tell how the toys in each group are alike.

   _____
   _____

   Tell how they are different.

   _____
   _____

4. Circle the toy that does not belong. Tell why.

   _____
   _____

   Name a toy that could be part of this group.

   _____
   _____

Grade 1 24 Chapter 4

4-2

Name _____

Problem-Solving Practice

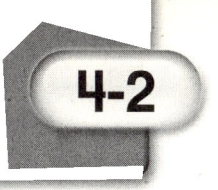

Picture Graphs

Use the graphs to answer the questions.

Amy's Coins					
pennies	🪙	🪙	🪙	🪙	🪙
nickels	🪙	🪙	🪙		
dimes	🪙	🪙			

Amy has pennies, nickels, and dimes.

1. Circle what Amy has the **most** of.

2. Circle what Amy has the **least** of.

3. How many more 🪙 than 🪙? _____

4. How many less 🪙 than 🪙? _____

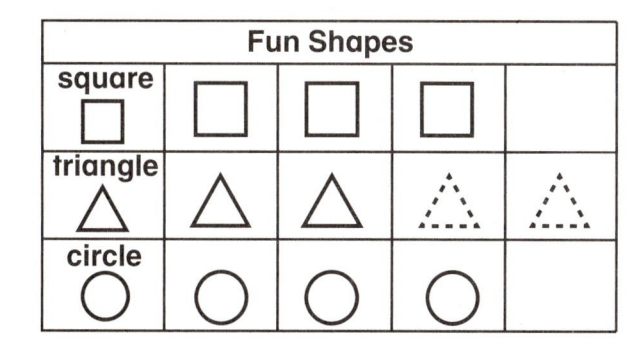

Fun Shapes				
square	□	□	□	
triangle	△	△	△	△
circle	○	○	○	○

5. Which row has the **fewest** shapes? Draw it.

_____

6. Add 2 △. Now which row has the **most** shapes?

_____

Grade 1   25   Chapter 4

4-4

Name _____

Problem-Solving Practice

Tally Charts

Use the tally charts.

1. Write each total in the chart.

2. What does this chart show?

   _____

Favorite Pets		
Pet	Tally	Total
🐟	||	
🐕	╫╫		
🐈	||||	

3. Which toy got the most votes?

   _____

4. How many voted for the robot?

   _____

Favorite Toys		
Toy	Tally	Total
robot	|||	3
bear	||	2
car	╫╫ ||	7

5. Ask your friends about their favorite fruit. Fill in the chart.

6. Write two questions about your chart.

Favorite Fruit		
Fruit	Tally	Total
apple		
banana		
orange		

_____

Grade 1   26   Chapter 4

4-5

Name _____

Problem-Solving Practice

Read a Bar Graph

Use the bar graph.

Snow Day Fun

Activity	Votes
Skating	3
Sledding	8
Making a snowman	5

0 1 2 3 4 5 6 7 8 9 10
Number of Votes

1. Which activity has fewer than 5 votes?

   _____

2. Don voted for the most popular activity. Which one did Don like most?

   _____

3. How many students in all voted for skating and making a snowman? Write a number sentence.

   _____ children

   _____

4. How many more students voted for sledding than for making a snowman? Write a number sentence.

   _____ children

   _____

5. How many people voted for a snowy day activity?

   _____

Grade 1   Chapter 4

4-6

Name _____

Problem-Solving Practice

Make a Bar Graph

Make a bar graph. Answer the questions.

Favorite Trip

zoo	▓	▓	▓			
museum	▓	▓	▓	▓	▓	
airport	▓	▓	▓	▓		

  0   1   2   3   4   5

---

1. Which trip got the fewest votes?

_____

2. How many more votes did the museum get than the zoo?

_____

3. How many students voted?

_____

4. Which two trips got a total of 7 votes?

_____

5. Which two trips got 8 votes in all?

_____

6. Which trip got fewer votes than the airport?

_____

Grade 1   28   Chapter 4

4-8

Name _____

Problem-Solving Practice

Certain or Impossible

Color the shapes to make the sentence true.

1. Picking a red square is certain.

   ☐ ☐ ☐ ☐

2. Picking a blue circle is impossible.

   ○ ○ ○ ○

3. Picking a green triangle is certain.

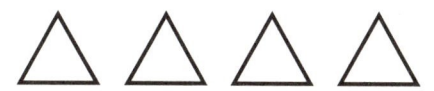

   △ △ △ △

4. Picking a red star is impossible.

   ☆ ☆ ☆ ☆

5. 🌼 🌼 🌼 🌼 🏈

   Mia picks an object from this row.
   Is she certain to pick a flower? Explain.

   _____

Grade 1   29   Chapter 4

5-1

Name _____

Problem-Solving Practice

Add in Any Order

Solve.

1. Julie sees 2 stars. Noah sees 3 stars. How many stars do they see in all?

   2 + 3 = ____   3 + 2 = ____

2. Draw stars to show your addition sentence from problem 1.

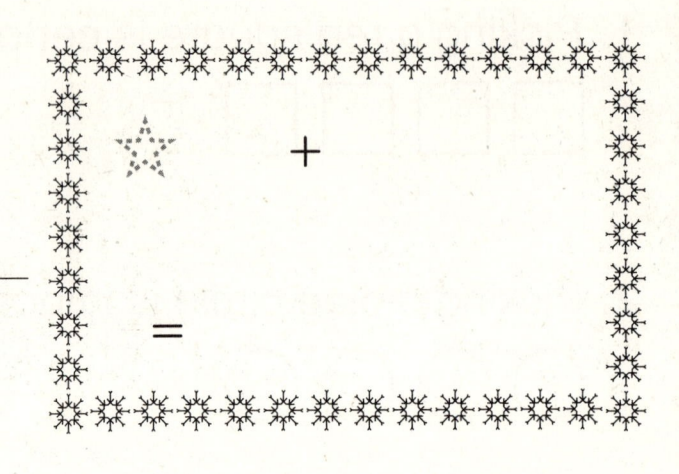

Solve. Write the addends.

3. Mom sees 2 bears at the zoo. Dad sees 1 bear. How many bears do they see in all?

   _____

   _____

4. One duck has 4 eggs. Another duck has 5 eggs. How many eggs in all?

   _____

   _____

5. Kim has 5 apples. She gets 1 more. How many apples does she have now?

   _____

   _____

6. Jill's flower has 5 leaves. It grows 4 more. How many leaves does it have now?

   _____

   _____

Grade 1 — Chapter 5

5-2

Problem-Solving Practice

Count on 1, 2, or 3

Use 🎲. Count on to find each sum.

1. Sally counts 3 shirts. She counts 3 more.

   3 + 3 = ____
           sum

2. Mark counts 8 socks. He counts 2 more.

   8 + 2 = ____
           sum

3. Jake saw 9 frogs. Then he saw 3 more. How many frogs did he see?

   9 + 3 = ____ frogs

4. Sandi saw 7 monkeys. Jan saw 2 monkeys. How many did they see?

      7
   + 2
   ─────
   ____ monkeys

5. A bus driver drove 8 miles. He stopped to eat. Then he drove 3 more miles. How many miles did he drive in all?

   ____ miles

6. 7 kids got on the bus. Then 3 more got on. Finally, 2 more got on. How many kids are on the bus now? Write the number sentence.

   ___ + ___ + ___ = ___

   ____ children

Grade 1   Chapter 5

Name _____

5-4 Problem Solving Practice

Add 1, 2, or 3

Circle the greater number. Count on to add.

1. 3 birds fly to a nest. 4 more birds fly to it. How many birds are in the nest?

    3 + 4 = _____

    _____ birds

2. 4 acorns are in a tree. 2 more are on the grass. How many total acorns are there?

    4 + 2 = _____

    _____ acorns

3. A butterfly is on a flower. 3 more are on the grass. How many butterflies are there?

    _____ + _____ = _____

    _____ butterflies

4. 6 bees are in a hive. 6 more fly in. How many bees are in the hive now?

    _____ + _____ = _____

    _____ bees

5. Joe catches 2 fish. Mom catches 5 fish. Dad catches 4 fish. How many fish do they catch?

    _____ + _____ + _____
    = _____ fish

6. Kevin and Lisa each see 2 bugs. Lo sees 4 bugs. How many total bugs do they see?

    _____ + _____ + _____
    = _____ bugs

Grade 1 — 32 — Chapter 5

5-5

Name _____

Problem-Solving Practice

Use a Number Line to Add

Use the number line to add. Write the number sentence.

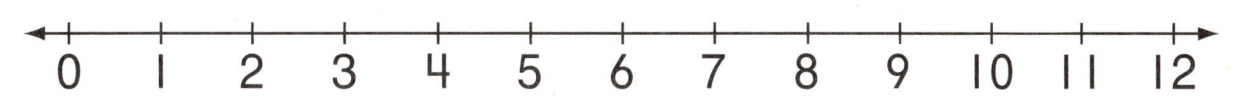

```
0  1  2  3  4  5  6  7  8  9  10  11  12
```

1. 6 🐦 are in the 🌿.
   1 new 🐦 flies to the 🌿.
   How many 🐦 in all?

   6 + 1 = _____ 🐦

2. 3 🐸 sit on a 🪵.
   2 more 🐸 sit.
   How many 🐸 in all?

   3 + 2 = _____ 🐸

3. 7 rabbits are on the lawn.
   2 rabbits are in the garden. How many rabbits in all?

   _____ + _____ = _____

   _____ rabbits

4. 8 nuts are in the bowl.
   Dad has 1 more. How many nuts are there?

   _____ + _____ = _____

   _____ nuts

5. Ann had 4 stickers. Bob gave her 2 more. Then Ann's mom gave her 2 more. How many stickers does Ann have now?

   ___ + ___ + ___ = ___

   _____ stickers

6. Gina found 8 shells. Abby found 2 shells. Jen found the same number as Abby. How many total shells did the girls find?

   ___ + ___ + ___ = ___

   _____ shells

Grade 1   Chapter 5

5-6

Name _____

Problem-Solving Practice

Doubles

Write the sum.

1. Sam has 3 books. Jody has 3 books. How many books are there?

   3 + 3 = _____ books

2. Jill has 2 shells. She finds 2 more. How many shells does she have now?

   2 + 2 = _____ shells

3. Kit has 4 stamps. His mom has 4 more. How many stamps do they have?

   4 + 4 = _____ stamps

4. Jake has 6 baseball cards. He gets 6 more. How many cards does he have in all?

   6 + 6 = _____ cards

5. Dara draws 5 pictures. Her friend draws the same number of pictures. How many pictures do they draw altogether?

   ___ + ___ = ___
   pictures

6. Sandi has 12 beads. Write a doubles fact that shows the number of beads she has.

   ___ + ___ = 12 beads

Grade 1　　　　　34　　　　　Chapter 5

5-7

Name _____

Problem-Solving Practice

Doubles Plus 1

Use doubles and doubles plus 1 facts. Solve.

1. Jessie sees 3 birds. Bill sees 4 birds.
   How many birds do they see?

   3 + 3 = ____   3 + 4 = ____ birds

2. There are 5 red flowers and 6 blue flowers.
   How many flowers in all?

   5 + 5 = ____   5 + 6 = ____ flowers

3. Becky colors with 4 crayons. Jeff uses 5 crayons.
   How many crayons do they have in all?

   ____ + ____ = 8   4 + 5 = ____ crayons

4. Paul has 1 pencil. He finds 2 more.
   How many pencils does he have now?

   ____ + ____ = 2   1 + 2 = ____ pencils

5. Mom packs 2 apples for lunch. Dad packs 3 more.
   How many apples do they pack in all?

   ____ + ____ = ____   ____ + ____ = ____ apples

6. 6 children play soccer. 7 children play baseball.
   How many children are playing?

   ____ + ____ = ____   ____ + ____ = ____ children

Grade 1   Chapter 5

6-1

Name _____

Problem-Solving Practice

Count Back 1, 2, or 3

Solve. Use 🎲.

1. Start at the number 7. Count back 2. What is the number?

   7, _____, _____

   7 − 2 = _____

2. Start at the number 4. Count back 3. What is the number?

   4, _____, _____, _____

   4 − 3 = _____

3. Ann runs for 10 minutes. Ray runs 3 fewer minutes than Ann. How many minutes does Ray run?

   10 − 3 = _____ minutes

4. John has 9 pencils. He uses 2 of them. How many pencils does John have now?

   9 − 2 = _____ pencils

5. Angel has 11 grapes. He gives 3 to his friend. How many grapes does he have left?

   11 − 3 = _____ grapes

6. Maggie has 6 balloons. She gives Jill one to take home. She gives Kathy one to take home. How many balloons does Maggie still left?

   6 − 2 = _____ balloons

Grade 1

Chapter 6

6-3

Name _____

Problem-Solving Practice

Use a Number Line to Subtract

Solve. Use the number line to count back.

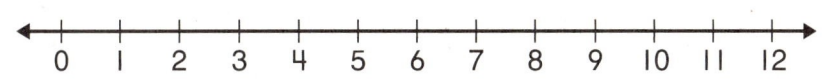

```
← 0  1  2  3  4  5  6  7  8  9  10  11  12 →
```

1. Start at the number 8. Count back 3. What is the number?

   _____

2. Don hits the ball 7 times. Tim hits the ball 2 times. How many more times does Don hit than Tim?

   $7 - 2 =$ _____ times

3. May jumps rope for 8 minutes. Liz jumps 2 fewer minutes. How many minutes does Liz jump?

   $8 - 2 =$ _____ minutes

4. Bert starts out with 12 marbles. He loses 3 of them. How many marbles does he have left?

   $12 - 3 =$ _____ marbles

5. Casey has 10 sticks of colored chalk. She gives Dean a green, a yellow, and a blue stick of chalk. How many sticks does Casey have now?

   _____ − _____ = _____

6. Start at number 9. Decrease that by 2. What's that number?

   $9 - 2 =$ _____

   Then subtract 3 more. What's the number now?

   _____ − _____ = _____

Grade 1   37   Chapter 6

6-5

Name _____

Problem-Solving Practice

Use Doubles to Subtract

Use doubles to solve.

1. Drew has 8 pens. He gives 4 of them to his sister. How many pens does Drew have now?

    8 – 4 = _____ pens

2. The school has 4 buses. 2 of them are yellow. How many are **not** yellow?

    4 – 2 = _____ buses

3. Jessie's dad has 6 pairs of jeans. He gives away 3. How many pairs of jeans are left?

    ____ – ____ = ____ jeans

4. There are 10 apples in the tree. 5 fall off. How many apples are still in the tree?

    ____ – ____ = ____ apples

5. Pat finds four shells on the beach. He takes half of them home. How many does he take home?

    ____ – ____ = ____ shells

6. Jen wins 8 tickets to the baseball game. She gives 4 to her brother. Then she gives 2 to her friend. How many tickets does Jen have left?

    ____ – ____ = ____

    ____ – ____ = ____

    ____ tickets

Grade 1   Chapter 6

6-6 Problem-Solving Practice

Relate Addition to Subtraction

Write the related facts.

1. 11 − 6 = ___

   11 − ___ = ___

   ___ + 6 = 11

   ___ + ___ = 11

2. 5 + 7 = ___

   7 + ___ = ___

   ___ − 7 = ___

   ___ − 5 = ___

Solve. Write the related facts.

3. This month, there are 11 sunny days. There are also 5 rainy days. How many more sunny days are there?

   11 − ___ = 5 sunny days

   ___ + ___ = 11

4. Jen marks 8 days on the calendar. Bill marks 4 days. How many more days does Jen mark than Bill?

   ___ − ___ = ___ days

   ___ + ___ = ___

5. Today is May 6. Joni's birthday is in 4 more days. When is Joni's birthday?

   May ___

   ___ + ___ = ___

   ___ + ___ = ___

   ___ − ___ = ___

   ___ − ___ = ___

6. Groundhog Day was February 2. If today is February 11, how many days has it been since Groundhog Day?

   ___ days

   ___ + ___ = ___

   ___ + ___ = ___

   ___ − ___ = ___

   ___ − ___ = ___

Grade 1 — Chapter 6

6-7

Name _____

Problem-Solving Practice

Fact Families

Solve. Then, complete the fact family.

1. Lee has 5 balloons.
   Sid has 6 balloons.
   How many balloons in all?

   ____ ballons

   5 + 6 = ____
   11 − 5 = ____
   6 + 5 = ____
   11 − 6 = ____

2. Liz sets out 7 cups.
   Jill sets out 5 cups.
   How many cups in all?

   ____ cups

   7 + 5 = ____
   12 − 5 = ____
   5 + 7 = ____
   12 − 7 = ____

3. There are 4 party hats on the table. 7 more hats are added. How many hats are there in all? ____

   4 + 7 = ____
   11 − 4 = ____
   7 + 4 = ____
   11 − 7 = ____

4. 8 children play Pin the Tail on the Donkey. 4 children play Go Fish. How many children play? ____

   8 + 4 = ____
   12 − 4 = ____
   4 + 8 = ____
   12 − 8 = ____

5. 9 children eat a cracker. 3 children eat a second cracker. How many crackers in all?

   ____ crackers

   ____ + ____ = ____
   ____ + ____ = ____
   ____ − ____ = ____
   ____ − ____ = ____

Grade 1   Chapter 6

7-1

Name _____

Problem-Solving Practice

Ordering Events

Circle the correct time.

1. morning   afternoon

   evening

2. morning   afternoon

   evening

Solve.

3. Jim comes home from school. Is it morning, afternoon, or evening?

   It is _____.

4. I eat dinner in the _____.

   Before dinner I _____ _____.

5. I get dressed for school in the _____.

   After school I _____ _____.

6. What does Jim do before and after he makes a sandwich? Write **before** or **after**.

   He eats the sandwich.

   _____

   He gets out the bread.

   _____

Grade 1 — Chapter 7

7-2

Name _____

Problem-Solving Practice

Time to the Hour

Use the clocks to solve.

1. Greg has a music lesson.
   What time is it? _____ o'clock.

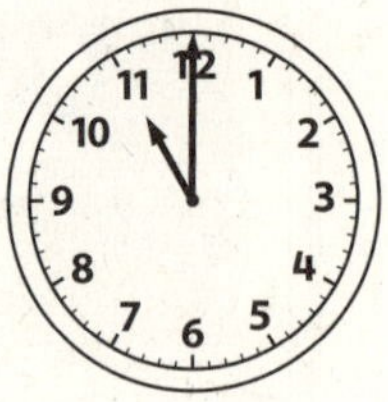

2. Jane has a dance lesson.
   What time is it? _____ o'clock.

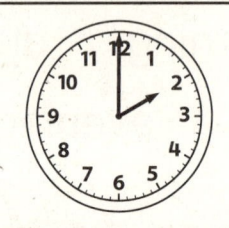

3. The time is 3 o'clock.
   Millie takes a nap for one hour.
   What time does her nap end?
   It ends at _____ o'clock.

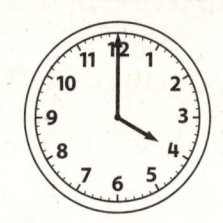

4. The time is 7 o'clock.
   David reads a story for one
   hour. What time does he stop?
   He stops at _____ o'clock.

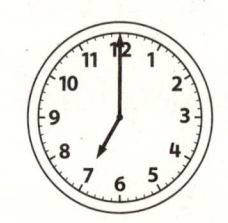

5. Lin has to leave at 9 o'clock.
   Should she leave now?
   Explain. _____

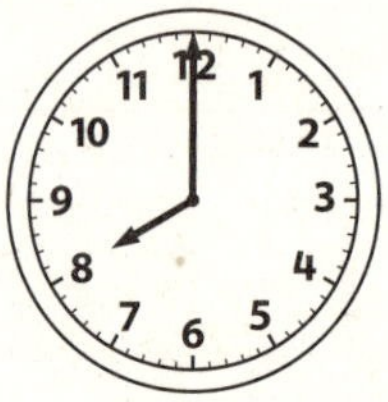

6. Eli's movie starts at 4 o'clock.
   Should he turn on the TV now?
   Explain. _____

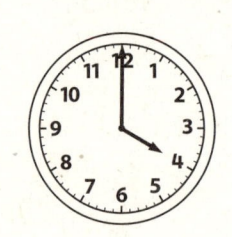

Grade 1   Chapter 7

7-3

Name _____

Problem-Solving Practice

Time to the Half Hour

Use the clocks to solve.

1. Tim wants to know what time it is.
   It is half past _____ .

2. The bus comes now. What time is it?
   It is half past _____ .

---

3. What time does Tanya eat dinner?
   half past _____

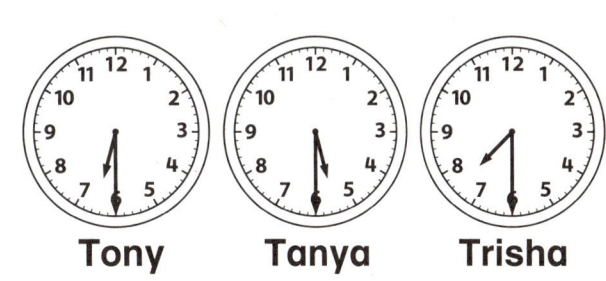

   Tony   Tanya   Trisha

4. What time does Tony eat dinner? half past _____

5. Terry eats dinner at the same time as Trisha. What time does Terry eat dinner?
   half past _____

6. Midge eats dinner one hour later than Tanya. What time does Midge eat dinner?
   half past _____
   Midge eats dinner at the same time as _____ .

Grade 1   43   Chapter 7

7-5

Name _____

Problem-Solving Practice

Telling Time to the Hour and Half Hour

Solve.

1. Eric has an art class at 11:00. Draw the time Eric's class meets.

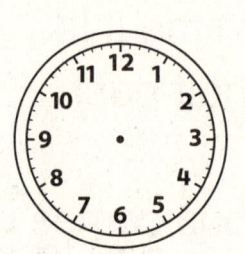

2. Maria has a dance lesson at 10:30. Draw the time Maria's lesson starts.

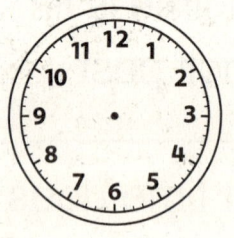

3. Carlos started walking at 3:00. He walked for a half hour. What time did he stop? _____ : _____

4. Beth went on a bike ride at 4:00. She biked for an hour. What time did she stop? _____ : _____

5. The hour hand points to 7. The minute hand points to 12. What time is it? _____ o'clock

6. The hour hand is between 9 and 10. The minute hand points to 6. What time is it?

_____

Grade 1   44   Chapter 7

7-6

Name _____

Problem-Solving Practice

Relate Time to Events

Solve.

1. Circle Carmen's longer activity.

2. Circle Rob's shorter activity.

3. Lena wrote a letter from 3:00 to 3:30. Then, she went ice skating from 4:00 to 5:30. Which activity took longer?
_____

4. Ms. Ito taught spelling from 10:00 to 10:30. Then, she taught math from 10:30 to 11:30. Which subject was shorter? _____

5. Sammy took pictures of squirrels from 8:00 to 8:30. Then, he took pictures of birds for an hour. Sammy took pictures of _____ longer.

6. Ned's muffins take a half hour to bake. His bread was in the oven from 2:30 to 3:30. Ned's _____ take a shorter time to bake.

Grade 1   45   Chapter 7

Name _____

8-1 Problem-Solving Practice

Counting to 20

Solve.

1. Karen has 10 peaches. Will has 5. Count on to find how many peaches they have. _____

2. April has 10 hats. Tammy has 3. Count on to find how many hats they have. _____

3. Brian has 7 marbles. How many more does he need to have 17? _____

4. Lisa has 10 bagels. How many more does she need to have 12? _____

5. Marc has 5 pears. Gina has 3 pears. How many more do they need to have 18? _____

6. Mary has 6 crayons. Flora has 4 crayons. How many more do they need to have 19? _____

8-2

Name _____

Problem-Solving Practice

Counting by Tens

Count by tens. Solve.

1. Matt has 4 sets of 10 trading cards. How many cards does he have?

   forty

2. Ashley has 6 sets of ten markers. How many markers does she have?

   sixty

3. Todd has 10 marbles. Chris has 10 marbles. Susan has 10 marbles. How many marbles are there in all?

   thirty

4. Ann and Beth each have 10 peas. How many peas do they have?

   twenty

5. Sara has 10 pencils. Jake, Joshua, Larry, and Michelle each have 10 pencils. How many total pencils are there?

   fifty

6. Don, Jerry, Ben, Tom, Terry, Sally, and Sam each have 10 flowers. How many flowers do they have?

   seventy

8-4

Name _____

Problem-Solving Practice

Hundred Chart

Use the hundred chart.

1	2	3	4	5	6	7	8	9	10
11	12	13	14	15	16	17	18	19	20
21	22	23	24	25	26	27	28	29	30
31	32	33	34	35	36	37	38	39	40
41	42	43	44	45	46	47	48	49	50
51	52	53	54	55	56	57	58	59	60
61	62	63	64	65	66	67	68	69	70
71	72	73	74	75	76	77	78	79	80
81	82	83	84	85	86	87	88	89	90
91	92	93	94	95	96	97	98	99	100

1. Kelly has one bean less than 18. How many does she have? _____ beans

2. Mark has 10 less than 44 blocks. How many blocks does he have? _____ blocks

3. Jasper has 75 coins. Mary has one more coin than Jasper. How many coins does Mary have?
_____

4. Amy has 10 fewer coins than Mary. How many coins does Amy have?
_____

5. Write the number of coins that Mary, Jasper, and Amy have in order. _____ _____ _____

Grade 1   Chapter 8

8-5

Name _____

Problem-Solving Practice

Estimating with Groups of Tens

Estimate. Then count to find the number.

1. Emma washes forks. How many?

   estimate: _____ forks

   count: _____ forks

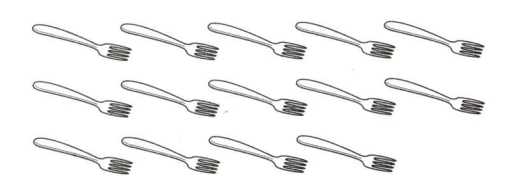

2. Next she washes spoons. How many?

   estimate: _____ spoons

   count: _____ spoons

3. Circle 10. Estimate. Then count.

   estimate: _____ count: _____

4. Circle 10. Estimate. Then count.

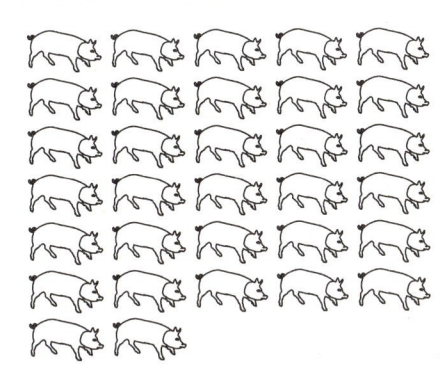

   estimate: _____ count: _____

5. Seth has 22 flowers. He gives away 10 flowers. How many are left?

   estimate: _____

   count: _____

6. Fran has 20 flowers. Dad gives her 16 more. How many are there in all?

   estimate: _____

   count: _____

Grade 1 — Chapter 8

8-7

Name _____

Problem-Solving Practice

Skip Counting by 2s, 5s, and 10s

Solve.

1. Ed skip counts by 2. He counted 2, 4, 6. What number is next?

   7   8   9

2. Jan skip counts by 5. She counted 5, 10, 15. What number is next?

   17   19   20

3. Trish counts by tens. Write the numbers she missed.

   10, _____, 30, _____, 50

4. Miles counts by fives. Write the numbers he missed.

   5, _____, 15, 20, _____

5. Pete skip counts: 10, 20, 30, 40, 50. How many does Pete count at a time? _____ What is the next number? _____

6. Greg counts his socks. He counts 2, 4, 6, 8, 10, 12. How many does Greg count each time? _____

Grade 1   Chapter 8

8-8

Name _____

Problem-Solving Practice

Skip Counting on a Hundred Chart

Use the chart to skip count.

51	52	53	54	55	56	57	58	59	60
61	62	63	64	65	66	67	68	69	70
71	72	73	74	75	76	77	78	79	80
81	82	83	84	85	86	87	88	89	90
91	92	93	94	95	96	97	98	99	100

1. Look at the numbers in the chart. Skip count by two. Circle the numbers as you count by twos.

2. Skip count by tens. Draw a box around the numbers as you count by tens.

3. Which numbers have a ○ and a □?

4. What pattern do you see for the numbers with a ○ and a □?

_____

5. Skip count by 5. What do the numbers have in common?

6. Lana skip counts to 100 by 5. Jim skip counts to 100 by 2. Who counts more numbers?

_____

Grade 1   51   Chapter 8

8-9

Name _____

Problem-Solving Practice

Even and Odd

Solve.

1. Reece says that 7 is an *even* number. Is he right? _____

2. Sofia thinks of a number between 20 and 22. Is it an *odd* or *even* number? _____

3. What are all the *even* numbers between 5 and 15? _____

4. Gina says that 19 is an *odd* number. Is she right? _____

5. Mr. Rice thinks of a number between 34 and 37. It is not 35. Is it an *odd* or *even* number?

   _____

6. Sunny Side Store sells 🖐. Do you think the store will have an *even* or *odd* number of 🖐?

   _____

   Why? _____

   _____

   _____

Grade 1   Chapter 8

9-1

Name _____

Problem-Solving Practice

Compare and Order Lengths

Solve. Use the flowers for 1–4.

1. Color the shortest flower red.

2. Color the longest flower blue.

3. Is the bug shorter or longer than the longest flower?

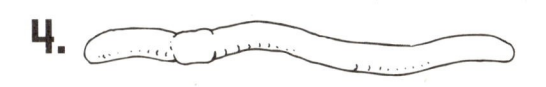

   _____

4. Is the worm shorter or longer than the shortest flower?

   _____

5. Marco starts at the door and takes 5 steps. Lisa starts at the door and takes 8 steps. Which person walked a longer length?

   _____

6. Han has a brush that is 4 paper clips long. Maggie has a brush that is 2 paper clips longer than Han's. Is Maggie's brush 2 paper clips long or 6 paper clips long?

   _____

9-2

Name _____

Problem-Solving Practice

Nonstandard Units of Length

Solve. Use the lines for 1–2.

1. Draw the shortest line.   2. Draw the longest line.

3. Estimate the length of the 〜〜 line.

   estimate: about _____ 📎 long

   measure: about _____ 📎 long

4. Estimate the length of the ⟋⟋⟋ line.

   estimate: about _____ 📎 long

   measure: about _____ 📎 long

5. Use 📎. Estimate how many 📎 long the bottom of this paper is. Then measure it.

   estimate: about _____ 📎 long

   measure: about _____ 📎 long

Grade 1   Chapter 9

9-4

Name _____

Problem-Solving Practice

Compare and Order Weights

Solve.

1. Which is heaviest? a marble, car, or book?

   _____

2. Which is lightest? a book, car, or marble?

   _____

3.  Is the balance correct? Which is heavier

   _____

4. 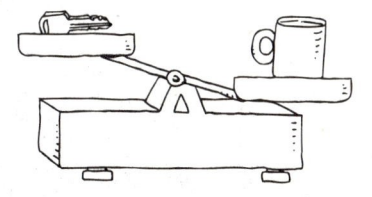 Is the balance correct? Which is lighter?

   _____

5. Circle the balance that shows that the book is lighter than the bucket.

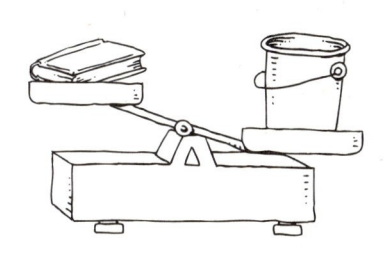

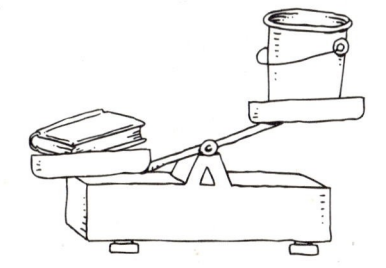

Grade 1   55   Chapter 9

9-5

Name _____

Problem-Solving Practice

Compare and Order Capacities

Answer the questions.

1. Chen has a can of soda. Brian has a bottle of soda. Who has more soda? _____

2. Ruth sees a cup, a bucket, and a barrel. Which holds the least? _____

3. Neil sees a car, a scooter, and a bus. Which can fit the most people? _____

4. Andy has a chair in his living room. Rob has a sofa in his living room. Which can more people sit on? _____

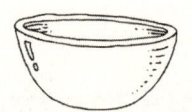

5. Curtis has a cup, a small bowl, and a large mixing bowl. They all have milk in them. Which has the least milk? _____

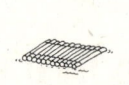

6. Mel sees a raft, a boat, and a ship on the water. They are all carrying people. Which holds the least? _____

Grade 1   56   Chapter 9

9-6

Name _____

Problem-Solving Practice

Compare and Order Temperatures

Read the questions. Circle the answers.

1. The 🍕 is _____ than the 🖍.

   hotter   colder

2. The 🍦 is _____ than the ☀.

   hotter   colder

3. The snowball is _____ than the baseball.

   hotter   colder

4. The popcorn is _____ than the milk.

   hotter   colder

Read the questions. Write the answers.

5. Pearl says the 🍞 is hotter than a 🎈. Is she right?

   _____

6. Name something that is colder than a lunchbox.

   _____

Grade 1   57   Chapter 9

9-8

Name _____

Problem-Solving Practice

Compare Areas

Read the questions. Write yes or no.

1. Do the 🥾 cover more area than the 🩴? _____

2. Does the 🌳 cover less area than the 🌰? _____

3. Does a house cover more area than a car? _____

4. Does a fish cover less area than a boat? _____

Write your answers.

5. Name something that takes up less area than a desk.

   _____

6. Name something that takes up more area than you.

   _____

Grade 1   Chapter 9

9-9

Name _____

Problem-Solving Practice

Order Areas

Draw the missing shapes.

1. ○   _____   ◯

2. △   △   _____

3. _____   □   ▫

Draw your own shapes. Order them from what covers the least to what covers the most.

4. _____   _____   _____

Grade 1   59   Chapter 9

10-1

Name _____

Problem-Solving Practice

Doubles

Solve by using doubles. Draw a picture.

1. Bo has 2 marbles. Lin has 2 marbles. How many marbles?

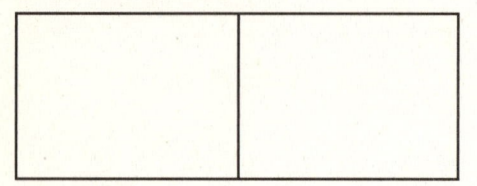

   2 + 2 = _____ marbles

2. Jo has 3 red flowers. Ken has 3 yellow flowers. How many flowers?

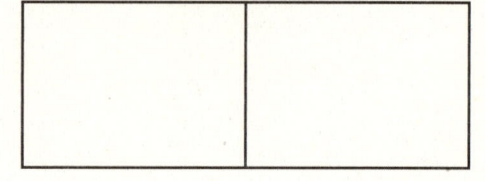

   3 + 3 = _____ flowers

3. Stan has 6 books. Jason has 6 books. How many books in all?

   _____ + _____ = _____
   books

4. I have 5 crayons. Lisa has the same number. How many crayons in all?

   _____ + _____ = _____
   crayons

5. Nina baked 12 cupcakes. She wants to give half of them to Sara. What double is in 12?

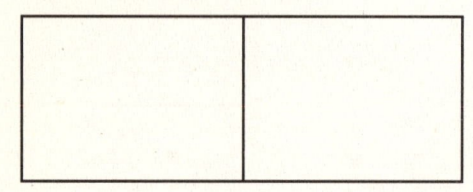

   _____ + _____ = 12

6. Chuck has 4 rockets. Dave has the same number. How many rockets in all?

   _____ rockets

   Andy has 3 more rockets. How many rockets now?
   _____ rockets

Grade 1 — Chapter 10

10-2

Name _____

Problem-Solving Practice

Doubles Plus 1

Use the doubles fact to help you solve.

1. Jen has 2 crayons. Lea has 3 crayons. How many crayons in all?

   2 + 2 = ____

   2 + 3 = ____ crayons

2. Noah drew 4 kites. Then he drew 5 more. How many kites did Noah draw?

   4 + 4 = ____

   4 + 5 = ____ kites

3. Tina has 5 ribbons. Bea has 6 ribbons. How many total ribbons do they have?

   ____ + ____ = 10

   5 + 6 = ____ ribbons

4. Glen drew 6 pictures. Ava drew 7 pictures. How many pictures did they draw in all?

   ____ + ____ = 12

   6 + 7 = ____ pictures

5. Millie has 8 cents. Ted has 9 cents. How many cents do they have altogether?

   ____ + ____ = ____

   ____ + ____ = ____ cents

Grade 1   Chapter 10

Name _____

10-3 Problem-Solving Practice

Make a 10 to Add

Make 10 to add. Use WorkMat 1 and ●○ to solve.

1. If $10 + 2 = 12$, what is
   $8 + 4 =$ _____

2. If $10 + 3 = 13$, what is
   $9 + 4 =$ _____

3. If $10 + 1 = 11$, what is
   $3 + 8 =$ _____

4. If $10 + 3 = 13$, what is
   $8 + 5 =$ _____

5. If $10 + 2 = 12$, what is
   $9 + 3 =$ _____

6. If $10 + 1 = 11$, what is
   $7 + 4 =$ _____

7. Spot has 9 sticks.
   Rex has 3 sticks.
   How many total sticks
   do they have?
   $9 + 3 =$ _____ sticks

8. Fluffy has 7 toys.
   Tiger has 4 toys.
   How many total toys do
   they have?
   $7 + 4 =$ _____ toys

9. Luke spends 9¢ for a treat for his dog.
   Sam spends 5¢ for a treat for his cat.
   How much do the children spend?
   _____ ¢ + _____ ¢ = _____ ¢

10. Andy spends 8¢ for a treat for his cat.
    Cory spends 3¢ less than Andy.
    How much do the two boys spend in all?
    _____ ¢ + _____ ¢ = _____ ¢

Grade 1   Chapter 10

10-5

Name _____

Problem-Solving Practice

Use Doubles to Subtract

Use doubles to solve. For 5–6, use the answers to crack the code.

1. What is the double fact that will help find the difference?

    $14 - 7 =$ _____

    ___ + ___ = ___

2. Find the subtraction fact for this double. What is it?

    $4 + 4 =$ _____

    ___ − ___ = ___

3. What is the double fact that will help find the difference?

    $16 - 8 =$ _____

    ___ + ___ = ___

4. Find the subtraction fact for this double. What is it?

    $9 + 9 =$ _____

    ___ − ___ = ___

5. $12 - 6 =$ ___ (d)

    $8 - 4 =$ ___ (g)

    $14 - 7 =$ ___ (w)

6. $16 - 8 =$ ___ (r)

    $10 - 5 =$ ___ (o)

    $18 - 9 =$ ___ (k)

$\underset{4}{g} \quad \underset{5}{o} \quad \underset{5}{\_} \quad \underset{6}{\_} \quad \underset{7}{\_} \quad \underset{5}{\_} \quad \underset{8}{\_} \quad \underset{9}{\_}$!

Grade 1   Chapter 10

10-6

Name _____

Problem-Solving Practice

Relate Addition and Subtraction

Solve.

1. Mike has 5 marbles. Jake has 6 marbles. How many marbles do the boys have in all? Use this as the addition fact:

    5 + 6 = _____ marbles

2. Write the related subtraction facts.

    11 – _____ = _____

    11 – _____ = _____

Mac has 9 red toy cars. He also has 5 blue toy cars.

3. How many toy cars does he have? Write the addition facts.

    _____ + _____ = _____

    _____ + _____ = _____

4. Write the related subtraction facts.

    _____ – _____ = _____

    _____ – _____ = _____

---

5. Joey read 8 books. May read 3 books. How many books did they read?

    addition fact:

    _____ + _____ = _____

    subtraction facts:

    _____ – _____ = _____

    _____ – _____ = _____

6. Chan has 3 goldfish. His sister has 9 goldfish. How many goldfish in all?

    addition fact:

    _____ + _____ = _____

    subtraction facts:

    _____ – _____ = _____

    _____ – _____ = _____

Grade 1   Chapter 10

10-8

Name _____

Problem-Solving Practice

Fact Families

Solve.

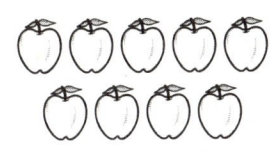

1. How many apples were picked? Count the apples.

   9 + 4 = _____

   4 + 9 = _____

2. Complete the fact family for the apples.

   13 − 4 = _____

   13 − 9 = _____

3. 6 students eat grapes. 5 students eat cheese. How many students eat in all?

   _____ students

   addition facts:

   _____ + 5 = _____

   _____ + 6 = _____

4. There are 14 cups of juice. Bill set out 6 cups. How many more cups are left?

   _____ cups

   subtraction facts:

   _____ − 6 = _____

   _____ − 8 = _____

Peter uses 7, 8, and 15 in his fact family.
Cori uses 9, 6, and 15 in her fact family.

5. Show Peter's facts.

   _____ + _____ = 15

   _____ + _____ = 15

   _____ − _____ = _____

   _____ − _____ = _____

6. Show Cori's facts.

   _____ + _____ = 15

   _____ + _____ = 15

   _____ − _____ = _____

   _____ − _____ = _____

Grade 1   Chapter 10

10-9

Name _____

Problem-Solving Practice

Ways to Model Numbers

Solve.

1. Circle the pictures that show ways to make 10.

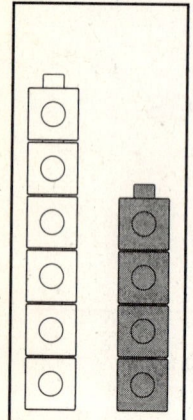

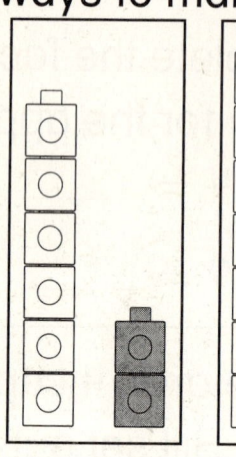

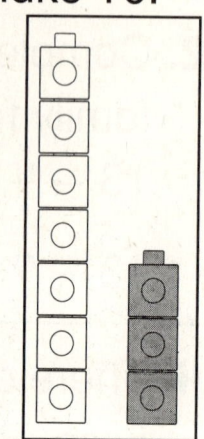

2. Jamie has red markers. Joni has blue markers. They have 7 in all. Circle the facts that show how many markers in all.

   6 + 1   5 + 2
   7 + 1   3 + 4

3. Joe beats his drum 12 times. Sara beats her drum 3 less times than Joe. How many times does Sara beat her drum? _____ times

   Write three different ways to show that sum.

   _____ ○ _____ = 9
   _____ ○ _____ = 9
   _____ ○ _____ = 9

4. The class has 9 big triangles and 3 small ones. How many triangles do they have in all? _____ triangles.

   Write three different ways to show that sum.

   _____ ○ _____ = 12
   _____ ○ _____ = 12
   _____ ○ _____ = 12

Grade 1   Chapter 10

11-1

Name _____

Problem-Solving Practice

Pennies and Nickels

Solve.

1. Andrea has 🪙🪙🪙🪙.

   How much does she have? _____ ¢

2. John has 10 pennies. He wants to trade for nickels. How many nickels can he get?

   _____ nickels

3. Which is more, 3 nickels or 2 nickels and 3 pennies?

   _____

   How do you know?

   _____

4. Millie has 🪙🪙.

   How much does she have? _____ ¢

5. Ben has 3 coins. He counts them. He has 11¢. What 3 coins does Ben have?

   _____

6. A toy costs 25¢. Rico has 4 nickels and 7 pennies. Can he buy the toy?

   _____

   How do you know?

   _____

Grade 1   67   Chapter 11

11-2

Name _____

Problem-Solving Practice

Pennies and Dimes

Solve.

1. Liam has [2 dimes and 4 pennies].

   What is the amount?

   _____ ¢

2. Write the amount for Lara's coins.

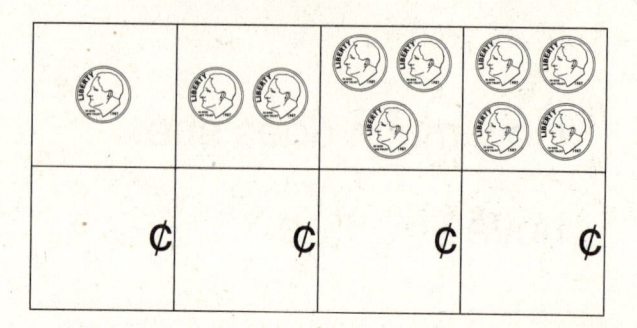

1 dime	2 dimes	3 dimes	4 dimes
_____ ¢	_____ ¢	_____ ¢	_____ ¢

3. Carol has 3 dimes. Nan has 1 dime and 8 pennies. How much money do they have in all?

   _____ ¢

4. Jiro has 1 dime. How many pennies can he get?

   1 dime = _____ pennies

5. Chuck has 60 pennies. He wants to trade for dimes. How many dimes can he get?
   60 pennies = _____ dimes

6. Juan has 70¢ in dimes and pennies. He has 6 dimes. How many pennies does he have?

   _____

7. 2 dimes = _____ pennies

8. 40 pennies = _____ dimes

9. 50 pennies = _____ dimes

10. 3 dimes = _____ pennies

11-3

Name _____

Problem-Solving Practice

Pennies, Nickels, and Dimes

Solve.

1. Fran used these coins to buy a book.

   How much did it cost?

   _____ ¢

2. A toy truck costs

   How much does it cost?

   _____ ¢

3. Dave has 37 pennies. He wants the fewest number of coins. How many dimes, nickels, and pennies does he trade for?

   _____   _____   _____

4. Lois has these coins.

   How much money does she have?

   _____ ¢

5. Ana has 3 coins. One of the coins is a dime. She has 20¢. What are the other 2 coins?

   _____

6. Greg has 6 nickels. He wants to trade for dimes. How many dimes can he get?

   _____ dimes

Grade 1   Chapter 11

11-4

Name _____

Problem-Solving Practice
Counting Money

Solve.

1. Mia has 3 🪙. Her sister has 4 🪙. How much do they have in all?
   _____ ¢

2. Jake buys a small car for 🪙🪙. He buys a toy cat for 🪙🪙. How much does he spend?
   _____ ¢

3. Vera counts her money.

   How much does she have? _____ ¢

4. Vera wants a toy plane. It costs 25¢. Which of her coins should Vera spend?

   _____

5. Donna has this much money.

   She wants to buy a toy bear. It costs 52 cents. Circle the coins she needs.

6. Donna buys the toy bear. How much does she have left? _____ ¢

   Write the number of coins she has left.

   _____ dime(s)

   _____ nickel(s)

   _____ penny(pennies)

Grade 1   70   Chapter 11

11-6

Name _____

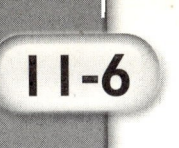

Problem-Solving Practice

Equal Amounts

Solve.

1. Ida has 15¢. If she had only nickels, how many would there be?
   _____ nickels

2. If she had dimes and pennies, how many would there be?
   _____ dime and _____ pennies

3. Alan has 25¢. If he had only pennies, how many would there be?
   _____ pennies

4. If he had only dimes and nickels, how many would there be?
   _____ dimes and _____ nickel

5. Pat has 5 nickels and 3 pennies.
   Greg has 1 dime and 8 pennies.
   What **one** coin does Greg need to have the same amount of money as Pat? Draw it.

6. Burt has 10 nickels. He earns 6 more nickels. How much money does Burt have now? _____
   How many dimes can he trade them for?
   _____

Grade 1   71   Chapter 11

11-7

Name _____

Problem-Solving Practice

Quarters

Solve.

1. Ava has 1 quarter and 1 nickel.
   She has _____ ¢.

2. Stan has 1 quarter. Ali has 2 dimes and 1 nickel. How much do they have in all?
   _____ ¢

3. Karen needs 85¢ to buy a pad of paper. She has 3 quarters. What coin does she need?
   _____

4. A bus ride costs a quarter and a dime.
   It costs _____ ¢.

5. Taro has 35¢ with only quarters and nickels. Draw the coins.

6. Jane has 2 quarters. She wants to buy crayons for 65¢. Jake gives her 2 coins. Now Jane has the exact amount. What 2 coins did Jake give her? Draw them.

Grade 1

Chapter 11

11-9

Name _____

Problem-Solving Practice

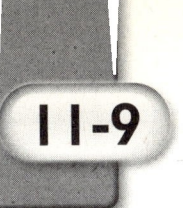

Money Amounts

Solve.

1. Sal has (quarter) and (nickel). [hat 28¢]

   Can he buy the hat? _____

2. A toy train costs 78¢. Kurt has 2 quarters. Kit has 1 quarter and 1 dime. Can they buy the train? _____

3. Dara has 2 quarters, 1 dime, and 2 pennies. She wants a balloon. The small balloon costs 36¢. The big balloon costs 65¢. Which can she buy?

   _____

4. Rob has (quarter) (dime) (nickel). [hockey stick 42¢]

   Can he buy the hockey stick? _____

5. Mark has 50¢. He has 2 of the same kind of coin. What are they? _____

6. Andy has 90¢. Each pack of cards costs one dime. How many packs of cards can he buy? _____

Grade 1   Chapter 11

12-1

Name _____

Problem-Solving Practice

Three-Dimensional Figures

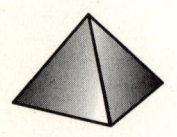

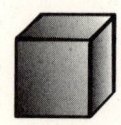

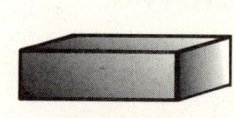

pyramid   cube   sphere   cone   cylinder   rectangular prism

Solve. Circle your answer.

1. Circle the objects that have curves.

2. Which objects do not have curves? Draw a box around each.

3. What three-dimensional figure is this object?

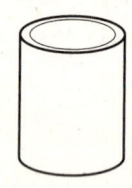

   cylinder   cone   pyramid

4. What three-dimensional figure is this object?

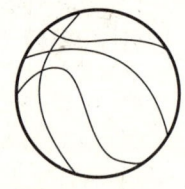

   cube   cylinder   sphere

5. What do a cone and a pyramid have in common?

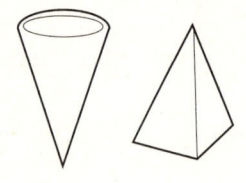

6. You want to build a wall. Which three-dimensional figure would you use to build it?

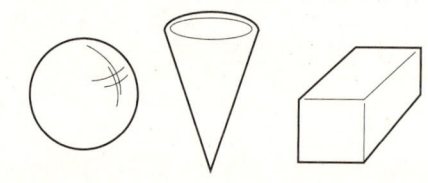

_____
_____

_____
_____

Grade 1   74   Chapter 12

12-2

Name _____

Problem-Solving Practice

Faces and Corners

Answer the questions.

1. Judy picks up an object with two faces. Circle the object.

2. Ron picks up an object with 8 corners. Circle the object.

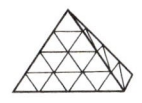

3. How many faces does the object have?

   _____

4. How many corners does the object have?

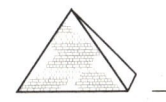

   _____

5. What two figures have the same number of faces?

   _____
   _____

6. What two figures have the same number of corners?

   _____
   _____

7. How are a cube and a rectangular prism alike?

   _____
   _____

Grade 1   75   Chapter 12

12-4

Name _____

Problem-Solving Practice

Two- and Three-Dimensional Figures

Look at the pictures. Then draw your own picture to solve.

1. Draw a picture of a two-dimensional figure.

2. Draw a picture of a three-dimensional figure.

3. Which of these figures has a ◯ face?

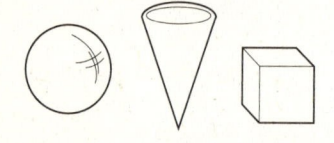

4. Which of these figures has 6 flat faces?

5. I am a two-dimensional figure. I have 3 corners and 3 sides. What figure am I?

6. I am a three-dimensional figure. I have 6 faces. Each face is a rectangle. What figure am I?

7. I am a three-dimensional figure. I have no faces and no corners. What figure am I?

8. I am a two-dimensional figure. I have 4 sides but they are not equal. What figure am I?

12-5

Name _____

Problem-Solving Practice

Two-Dimensional Figures

Answer the questions.

1. Tess drew a figure that has no sides. What figure did she draw? Circle it.

   □ △ ○

2. Quinn drew a figure that has 4 straight sides. Which figure did he draw? Circle it.

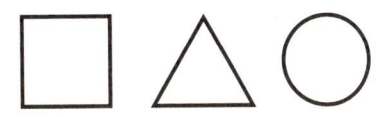

   □ △ ○

3. Betty drew a triangle and a square. Then she circled the figure with the least sides. Draw the figure that she circled.

4. Hana drew a rectangle and a square. Then she circled the figure that has two different lengths of sides. Which figure did she circle? Draw it.

5. Sam drew a figure. He used a ruler to draw. Circle the figure that he could *not* have drawn.

   ○ △ □

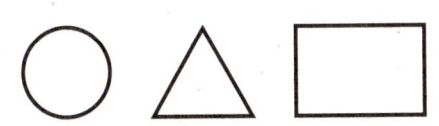

6. Jerry drew a figure. He used a ruler to draw four lines. Circle the figure that he could *not* have drawn.

   □ △ ▭

Grade 1   77   Chapter 12

12-7

Name _____

Problem-Solving Practice

Make New Figures

Use pattern blocks to solve. Write or draw your answers.

1. Lara says she can make a ▢ from a ▭ and a ▭. Is she right?

    _____

2. Gary says he can make a ○ from a △ and a ▢. Is he right?

    _____

3. Candy makes a ▭ from a ▢ and a ▢. She says this is the only way to make a ▭. Is she right?

    _____

4. Amata makes a ⬡ from a ⬠ and a ⬠. She says this there is another way to make a ⬡. Is she right?

    _____

5. Marcus tried to make a triangle using the shapes below. He is wrong. One shape is missing. Draw it.

    △ ▭
    △

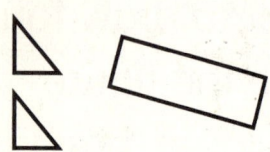

6. Miki tried to make a rectangle using the shapes below. She is wrong. One shape is missing. Draw it.

    ◁ ◇

_____   _____

Grade 1   Chapter 12

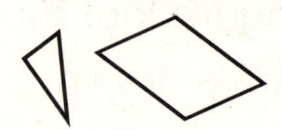

12-8

Name _____

Problem-Solving Practice

Position

Mrs. Robin shared this picture with her class.

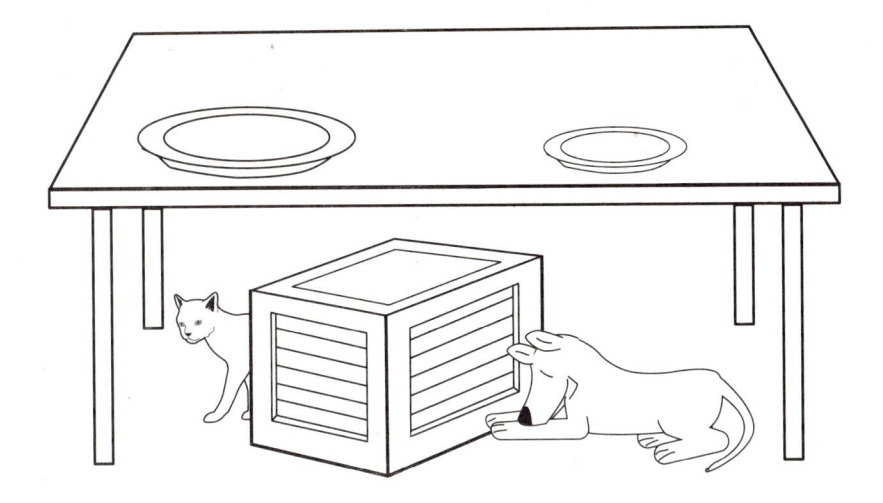

1. Is the cat behind the box or in front of the box?

   _____

2. Is the dog beside the table or under the table?

   _____

3. Draw a tree **to the right** of the table.

4. Draw a napkin **to the left** of the small plate on the table.

5. Draw a spoon **next to** the large plate. Did you draw the spoon on the right or the left?

   _____

6. Draw a bone **in front of** the dog. What is above the dog?

   _____

Grade 1   Chapter 12

12-9

Name _____

Problem-Solving Practice

Give and Follow Directions

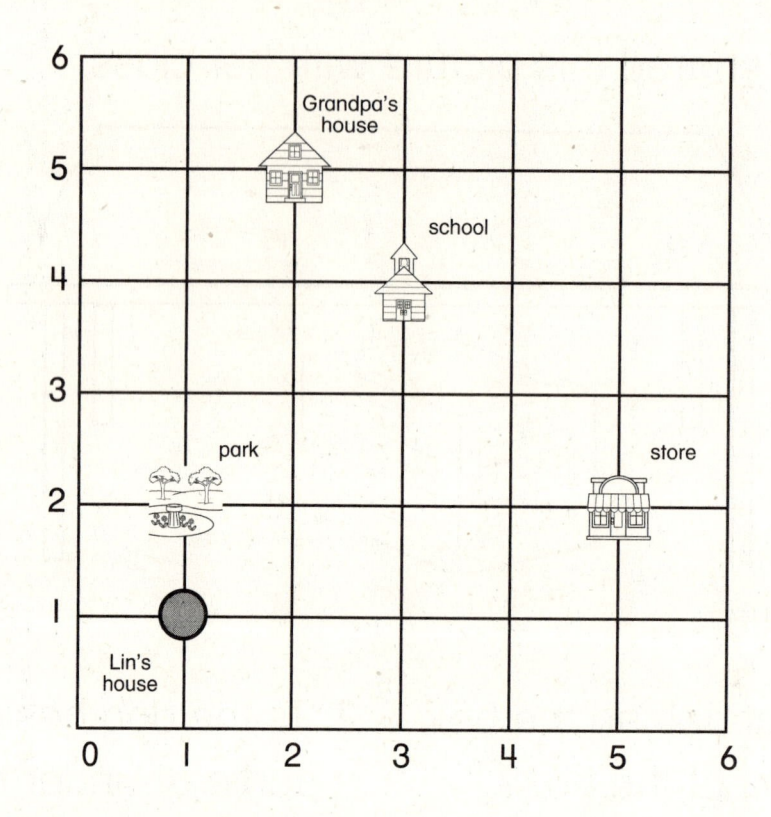

Answer the questions.

1. Lin is going to school. She starts at her house at ◯. Then she walks 2 blocks to the right. How many blocks up is her school? _____

2. Lin's mom is going to store. She starts at ◯. Then she walks 1 block up. How many blocks to the right is the store? _____

3. Lin goes to the park. She starts at ◯. How can she get to the park from there? _____

4. Lin's mom visits Grandpa. She starts at ◯. How can Mom get to Grandpa's house from there?

_____

Grade 1   80   Chapter 12

13-1

Name _____

Problem-Solving Practice

Tens

Solve.

1. Count by 10. Fill in the missing numbers.

   10, 20, 30, _____, 50, 60, _____, 80, 90, 100

2. Count groups of 10. Write the number.

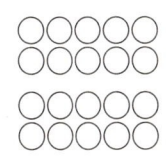

   _____ tens

   _____ circles

3. There are 3 vases. Each vase has 10 flowers. How many tens? How many flowers in all?

   _____ tens

   _____ flowers

4. There are 4 boxes. Each box has 10 buttons in it. How many tens? How many buttons in all?

   _____ tens

   _____ buttons

5. Sal has 8 bags. There are 10 marbles in each bag. How many total marbles are there?

   _____ marbles

6. Jenn has 50 crayons. She puts 10 crayons in each box. How many boxes does she have?

   _____ boxes

Grade 1   Chapter 13

13-2

Name _____

Problem-Solving Practice

Tens and Ones

Solve.

1. Count the stars.

    ☆☆☆☆☆
    ☆☆☆☆☆
    ☆☆☆☆☆
    ☆☆☆

    How many tens? _____
    How many ones? _____
    How many stars in all?

    _____ stars

2. Count the suns.

    ○○○○○○○○○○
    ○○○○○○○○○○
    ○○○○○○○○○○
    ○○○○○○

    How many tens? _____
    How many ones? _____
    How many suns in all?

    _____ suns

3. How is 65 different from 56? Use tens and ones to explain.

    _____

    _____

4. Mina has 20 logs in one box. She has 5 logs in another box. How many logs does she have in all?

    _____ ones

    _____ tens _____ ones

5. Jo is thinking of a number. It has 7 tens and 3 ones. What is the number?

    _____

6. Van's number is 2 tens less than Jo's number. What is Van's number?

    _____

Grade 1   Chapter 13

13-4

Name _____

Problem-Solving Practice

Numbers to 50

Solve. Show your answer two ways.

1. Hans had 12 toy cars.
   He got 5 more.
   How many toy cars does Hans have now?

   _____ tens _____ ones

   Write: _____

2. Ed has 36 pencils. Nate has 10 pencils. How many pencils do they have in all?

   _____ tens _____ ones

   Write: _____

3. Beth has 20 dolls. Sugi has 10 and Eva has 9. How many dolls do they have in all?

   _____ tens _____ ones

   Write: _____

4. Andy had 40 apples.
   He gave 9 to Nina and 10 to Vic.
   How many apples does he have left?

   _____ tens _____ ones

   Write: _____

5. Ali had 23 baseball cards. His dad gave him 2 more packs with 10 cards in each pack. How many cards does Ali have now?

   _____ tens _____ ones

   Write: _____

6. Brian has 27 comic books. His sister has 3 sets of 10 comic books. How many total comic books do they have?

   _____ tens _____ ones

   Write: _____

Grade 1   Chapter 13

13-5

Name _____

Problem-Solving Practice

Numbers to 100

Circle the answer.

1. 1 ten 3 ones

   13   twelve

2. 42

tens	ones
2	4

   4 tens 2 ones

Show your answer two different ways.

3. Frank has 30 stamps. He buys 5 more. How many stamps does Frank have now?

   _____ tens   _____ ones

   _____ stamps

4. Jin puts 85 beads in a jar. Sue takes 10 beads out. How many beads are in the jar?

   _____ tens   _____ ones

   _____ beads

5. Rhonda puts 20 books on a red shelf. Then she puts 10 books on a blue shelf and 4 books on a green shelf. How many books does Rhonda put away?

   _____ tens   _____ ones

   _____ books

6. Brad has 48 books. He gives 5 to his sister and 10 to his brother. How many books does Brad still have?

   _____ tens   _____ ones

   _____ books

13-6

Name _____

Problem-Solving Practice

Estimate Numbers

Answer the questions.

1. Cam invites 10 people to a party. June invites 8 people. Estimate how many people are invited to the party. _____
Write the exact number.

   _____

2. There are 2 rows of 10 cars. The third row has 4 cars. Estimate how many cars there are. _____
Write the exact number.

   _____

3. Cora has 6 dolls. Joe has 10 dolls. Sumi has 10 dolls. Estimate how many dolls they have. _____
Write the exact number.

   _____

4. Mia has 10 cousins. Kim has 20 cousins. Matt has 9 cousins. Estimate how many cousins they have in all. _____
Write the exact number.

   _____

5. Evan has 10 crackers. Paco has 20 crackers. Jin has 30 crackers. Liz has 7. Estimate how many crackers they have.

   _____

   Write the exact number.

   _____

6. The theater has 10 rows with 10 seats in each row. During the show, every seat was full except for 2. Estimate how many people were at the show.

   _____

   Write the exact number.

   _____

Grade 1   Chapter 13

13-8

Name _____

Problem-Solving Practice

Compare Numbers to 100

Solve. Circle the true statement. Then write > or <.

1. Mack's dog knows 9 tricks.
   Bo's dog knows 7 tricks.

   9 is greater than 7.
   9 is less than 7.
   9 ◯ 7

   9   7

2. Anya has 12 pictures.
   Gary has 21 pictures.

   12 is greater than 21.
   12 is less than 21.
   12 ◯ 21

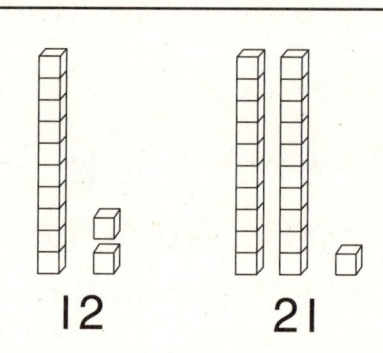

   12   21

Solve.

3. Beth's puppy is 26 days old. Ron's puppy is 18 days old.
   26 ◯ 18

4. A box of *Yums* has 23 dog treats. A box of *Tasty* has 32 dog treats.
   23 ◯ 32

5. Tad walks his dog for 45 minutes. Sam walks his dog for 28 minutes. Who walks longer?

6. Barry spends 78 cents on a leash. Adam spends 94 cents. Who spends more?

Grade 1   86   Chapter 13

13-9

Name _____

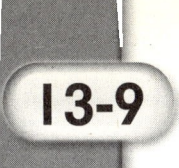

Problem-Solving Practice

Order Numbers to 100

Solve. Circle the answer.

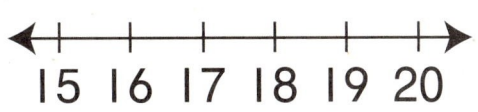

15 16 17 18 19 20

1. 16 is _____ 17.

   just before   just after

2. 19 is _____ 18.

   just before   just after

Write the numbers in the boxes.

3. What number comes between?

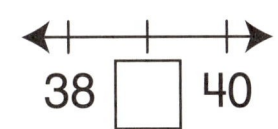

   38 ☐ 40

4. What number comes before? What number comes after?

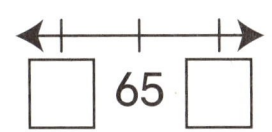

   ☐ 65 ☐

Solve.

5. Dave made a number line, but it is wrong.

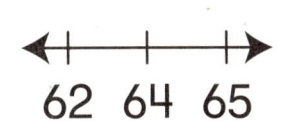

   62 64 65

   Fix Dave's number line.

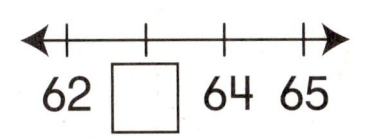

   62 ☐ 64 65

6. I am just after 88. What number am I? _____
   I am just before 90. What number am I? _____
   I am between 88 and 90. What number am I? _____

Grade 1 — 87 — Chapter 13

14-1

Name _____

Problem-Solving Practice

Equal Parts

Solve. Use pattern blocks to help.

1. Lily draws this picture. She says it has 2 equal parts. Is she right?

   _____

2. Tim draws a square. He wants 3 equal parts. Draw lines to show 3 equal parts.

3. Jose draws this picture. He says it has 3 equal parts. Is he right?

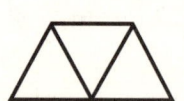

   _____

4. Calvin draws a triangle. He wants 4 equal parts. Draw lines to show 4 equal parts.

Grade 1   Chapter 14

14-3

Name _____

Problem-Solving Practice

One Half

Solve.

1. Joey has a hot dog. He eats $\frac{1}{2}$. His sister eats the other half. Joey says they had the same amount. Is he right?

   _____

2. Wendell eats $\frac{1}{2}$ a corn dog. A friend eats some of the rest, but not all of it. Wendell says his friend had more. Is he right?

   _____

3. Tina draws a square. Then she colors some of it.

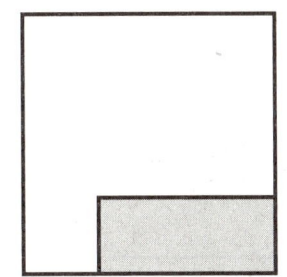

   She says she colored half. Is she right?

   _____

4. Kitty makes a sandwich. She cuts it in half. She eats one half. She gives the other half to 2 friends.

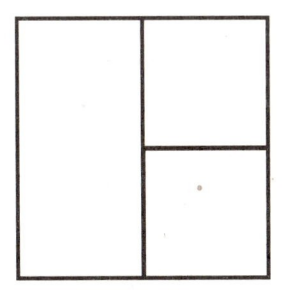

   Kitty says they all have an equal share. Is she right?

   _____

Grade 1   Chapter 14

14-4

Name _____

Problem-Solving Practice

One Third and One Fourth

Solve.

1. Heather has a hamburger. She eats $\frac{1}{3}$. Her brother eats the rest. Heather says her brother ate more. Is she right?

   _____

2. Warren shares a sandwich with 3 friends. Each eats an equal share. Warren says they each ate $\frac{1}{3}$ of the sandwich. Is he right?

   _____

3. Bart draws a triangle. Then he draws lines on it.

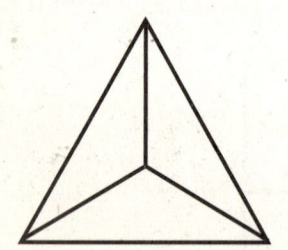

   He says he split the triangle into thirds. Is he right?

   _____

4. Zoe draws a rectangle. Then she draws some lines on it.

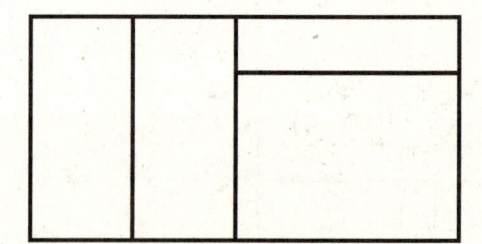

   Zoe says she split the rectangle into fourths. Is she right?

   _____

Grade 1   Chapter 14

14-5

Name _____

Problem-Solving Practice

Non-Unit Fractions

Solve.

1. Lynn has a sheet of paper. She tears it into 4 parts and shares them with friends. She says each part is $\frac{2}{3}$. Is she right?

   _____

2. Gordon colors a shape. If he colors $\frac{4}{4}$ of the shape, how much of the object would be shaded?

   _____

3. Mike draws a shape. Then he draws lines on it.

   He says that $\frac{2}{4}$ is the same as $\frac{1}{2}$.
   Is he right?

   _____

   How do you know?

   _____
   _____
   _____

4. Lois draws a shape. Then she draws lines on it.

   Lois says her picture shows $\frac{5}{4}$. Is she right?

   _____

   How do you know?

   _____
   _____
   _____

Grade 1   91   Chapter 14

14-6

Name _____

Problem-Solving Practice

Fractions of a Set

Solve.

1. Ben says that 4 out of 4 is the same as $\frac{4}{4}$. Is he right?

   _____

2. Doris counts 7 trees. 3 of them are in her yard. What fraction shows how many trees are in her yard?

   _____

3. Marta sees 9 animals at the pet store. She sees 4 rabbits and 5 cats. What fraction shows how many cats?

   _____

4. Kin says that 2 out of 4 is the same as $\frac{3}{4}$. Is he right?

   _____

5. Rich counts 6 ducks in the pond. 1 flies away. What fraction shows how many fly away?

   _____

6. Pam counts 4 apples. She eats 1. What fraction shows how many apples are left?

   _____

15-1

Name _____

Problem-Solving Practice

Add and Subtract Tens

Solve. Use ▭ to help.

1. Lily has 5 tens. She counts back 2 tens. How many are left?

   5 tens − 2 tens = _____ tens   50 − 20 = _____

2. Tim has 50 crayons. He gets 20 more. How many crayons does he have now?

   _____ + _____ = _____ crayons

3. Jose counts 20 blue bugs, 30 red bugs, and 10 yellow bugs. How many bugs does he count in all?

   _____ ◯ _____ ◯ _____ = _____ bugs

4. Calvin has 3 tens and 4 tens. How many does he have?

   3 tens + 4 tens = _____ tens   30 + 40 = _____

5. Flora has 40 apples. She eats 10 of them. How many apples are left?

   40 ◯ 10 = _____ apples

Grade 1   Chapter 15

15-2

Name _____

Problem-Solving Practice

Add with Two-Digit Numbers

Use the number line. Add to solve.

1. ←—+—+—+—+—+—+—+—+—+—+—→
    40 41 42 43 44 45 46 47 48 49 50

    Put your finger on 42. Count on 3.

    What is the number? _____

2. ←—+—+—+—+—+—+—+—+—+—+—→
    50 51 52 53 54 55 56 57 58 59 60

    Start at 52. Count on two. Then count on three more.

    What is the number? _____

3. ←—+—+—+—+—+—+—+—+—+—+—→
    70 71 72 73 74 75 76 77 78 79 80

    Start at 78. Count on 1. What is the number? _____

4. 25 kids are in the library. Then 3 more come.
   How many kids are in the library now? _____ kids

5. 45 books are on a shelf. Jill puts 2 more books on the shelf.
   How many books are there now? _____ books

6. Mrs. Lee buys 32 hot dog buns on Friday. She buys eight more on Monday.
   How many hot dog buns does she buy? _____ buns

Grade 1   Chapter 15

15-4

Name _____

Problem-Solving Practice

Add Two-Digit Numbers

Solve.

1. Mac walks 12 blocks to school. Jody walks 14 blocks. How many blocks do they walk in all?

   _____ + _____ = _____ blocks

2. Raul has 21 toy cars. He gets a set of 35 cars for his birthday. How many cars does he have now?

   _____ + _____ = _____ cars

3. 44 frogs, 21 fish, and 23 bugs live in a pond. How many bugs and frogs are there?

   _____ bugs and frogs

4. One farm has 21 pigs. The other farm has 44 pigs. How many pigs are there in all?

   _____ + _____ = _____ pigs

5. Rosa finds 36 ants outside. She finds 11 more in the shed. How many ants does she find?

   _____ ants

6. Leo has 13 red crayons, 24 blue crayons, and 45 yellow crayons. How many blue and yellow crayons does Leo have?

   _____ blue and yellow crayons

15-5

Name _____

Problem-Solving Practice

Estimate Sums

Estimate to solve.

1. Mr. Smith has 11 cents. Mrs. Smith has 19 cents. About how much do they have?

   _____ + _____ = _____   They have about _____ cents.

2. Mike's dad got 29 letters this week. He got 21 letters last week. About how many letters did he get?

   _____ + _____ = _____   He got about _____ letters.

3. Ella found 9 acorns in the yard. She found 27 acorns at the park. She says she has about 30 acorns.

   Is she right? _____   How do you know? _____ + _____ =

4. Mike has 9 cents. Rita has 31 cents. About how much do they have?

   _____ + _____ = _____   They have about _____ cents.

5. Suzie looked at the pictures in 24 books last month. She looked at 19 books this month. About how many books has she looked at?

   _____ + _____ = _____

   She looked at about _____ books.

Grade 1 — Chapter 15

15-6

Name _____

Problem-Solving Strategy

Subtract with Two-Digit Numbers

Subtract to solve. Use the number lines.

1. Put your finger on 67. Count back 4. What is the number? _____

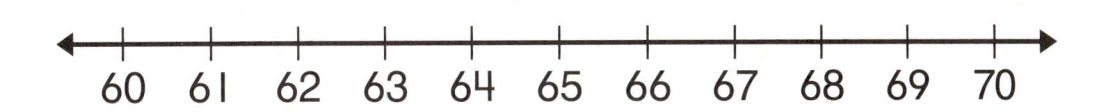

<-|---|---|---|---|---|---|---|---|---|---|->
  60 61 62 63 64 65 66 67 68 69 70

2. Jim starts at 29. He counts back four. Then he counts back four more. What is Jim's number? _____

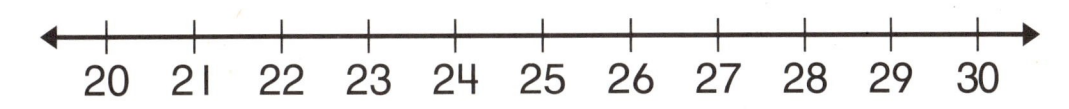

<-|---|---|---|---|---|---|---|---|---|---|->
  20 21 22 23 24 25 26 27 28 29 30

3. Lori starts at 24. She counts back 2. What is Lori's number? _____

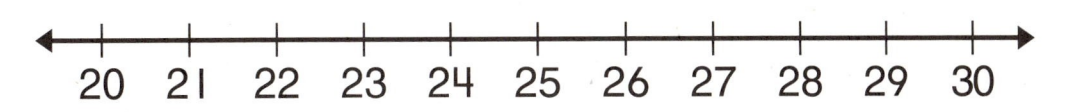

<-|---|---|---|---|---|---|---|---|---|---|->
  20 21 22 23 24 25 26 27 28 29 30

4. Jake has 47 baseball cards. He gives 5 to his friends. How many cards are left? _____ cards

5. Tina is 48 inches tall. Her brother is 6 inches shorter than Tina. How tall is Tina's brother? _____ inches tall

6. Mr. Watson made 39 sandwiches. He sold three on the first day. He sold four on the second day. How many sandwiches does he have left? _____ sandwiches

Grade 1   Chapter 15

15-7

Problem-Solving Practice

Subtract Two-Digit Numbers

Subtract to solve.

1. Tia is 49 inches tall. Her brother is 35 inches tall. How much taller is Tia?

    _____ − _____ = _____

    Tia is _____ inches taller than her brother.

2. Jill has 56 coins. She loses 22 of them. How many coins are left? _____ coins

3. 63 crows sit on a fence. 30 fly away. Then 21 more fly away. How many crows are still on the fence? _____

4. Paco runs for 39 minutes. His sister runs for 11 minutes. How many more minutes does Paco run?

    _____ − _____ = _____

    Paco runs for _____ more minutes than his sister.

5. A library has 67 books. 42 books are checked out. How many books are left? _____ books

6. Ms. May has 88 cents. She gives 13 cents to her son. She gives 25 cents to her daughter. How much does Ms. May have left? _____ cents

15-9

Problem Solving Practice

Estimate Differences

Estimate to solve.

1. Cal has 21 cents. His brother has 9 cents. About how much more does Cal have?

   _____ − _____ = _____

   Cal has about _____ cents more.

2. Ann has 47 game cards. She gives 21 cards to her friends. About how many cards does she have now?

   _____ − _____ = _____   She has about _____ cards.

3. Rosa runs for 45 minutes the first day. She runs 23 minutes the next day. She says she ran about 70 minutes in all.

   Is she right? _____

4. Jun's mom buys 45 apples. Jun eats 8 of them. About how many apples are left?

   _____ − _____ = _____

   There are about _____ apples left.

5. Nate catches 28 fish. Tina catches 66 fish. Tina says she has about 50 more fish than Nate. Nate says she only has about 40 more.

   Who is right? _____